THE NEW

Alaska Cookbook

THE NEW

Alaska
Cookbook

RECIPES FROM
THE LAST FRONTIER'S
BEST CHEFS

Kim Severson
with Glenn Denkler

 SASQUATCH BOOKS
SEATTLE

Printed in Canada
Distributed by Publishers Group West
12 11 10 09 08 07   12 11 10 9 8 7 6

Cover and interior design: Kate Basart
Cover and interior photographs: Hayden Photography
Composition: Brian Owada
Copy editor: Susan Derecskey
Proofreader: Sigrid Asmus
Indexer: Miriam Bulmer

Library of Congress Cataloging in Publication Data
Severson, Kim
The new Alaska cookbook : recipes from the last frontier's best chefs / by Kim Severson, with Glenn Denkler.
          p.   cm.
Includes index.
ISBN 1-57061-269-2
1. Cookery, American. 2. Cookery—Alaska. I. Denkler, Glenn. II. Title.

TX715 .S1462 2001
641.59798—dc21

Sasquatch Books
119 South Main Street, Suite 400
Seattle, Washington 98104
(206) 467-4300
www.sasquatchbooks.com
custserv@sasquatchbooks.com

Contents

Recipe List

Acknowledgments

Thanks first to the chefs who happily donated their time and recipes. Thanks also to the editors at Sasquatch for understanding why this book was important and to my editors and colleagues at both the *Anchorage Daily News* and the *San Francisco Chronicle*. A high-five to Glenn Denkler for his professionalism and friendship, and a special thank you to my partner, Kim Wyatt, for her smart edits and her loving encouragement.

—*Kim Severson*

The recipes submitted were stunning to the palate and fun to test. Thanks to the chefs for their time and talent. I needed a lot of support in the writing and testing of these recipes. For her patience and understanding for the time that I spent away from her, I most appreciate the love of my wife, Sheryl Davis. For the discerning taste buds and full stomachs, I thank the guinea pigs for all of the recipes tested: Bill Davis, Ken Morris, Tim Doebler, Clarence Davis, Tina Joseph, Dilys Roblin, Rachel Yould, Brett Yould, Sharon Macklin, Jerry Reber, and Sheryl. A tip of the toque to Kim Severson: not only a good friend, but also the best darned food writer in the universe.

—*Glenn Denkler*

Introduction

I spent almost eight years as a journalist in Alaska, writing often about the state's food and restaurants. Here in San Francisco, a place many argue is the epicenter of the American food scene, people find that funny. "Lots of whale blubber recipes?" they ask.

OK, so there was whale blubber—in particular, a potluck featuring pink and black cubes of maktak (pronounced *muk-tuk*) that had been dipped in seal oil. Unless a group of Inupiat Eskimos are coming over for dinner, I wouldn't recommend it as a great party dish.

But there were plenty of glorious food moments, and those are the ones I describe to people who can't imagine what it's like to cook and eat in America's largest, coldest, and most remote state.

I tell them about a snowy Sunday afternoon in a friend's kitchen, watching a man who wrestles 400-pound crab pots out of the Bering Sea for a living dunk King crab legs in a big pot of boiling water. These weren't the anemic crab legs of cut-rate ocean cruises and Vegas buffets. The crab legs were close to two feet long and dense with batons of sweet meat. He piled them in the stainless steel sink, and we spent the afternoon leaning against the kitchen counters, cutting open the shells with scissors. We would occasionally dip chunks of the snowy white meat into a little pan of hot clarified butter, but the crab was so sweet it tasted best straight from the salty red shell.

Or I describe a summer morning on the Little Susitna River. At 4 A.M. the sun was already strong. Using a combination of good advice and dumb luck, I pulled a 35-pound King salmon out of the river. We cut thick slices from the red fillets and grilled them with nothing but olive oil, salt, and pepper. We ate it for breakfast, and it was so good I thought Americans would readily give up bacon if they could get just one bite of this fish.

Alaskans who love food—especially professional chefs—live for those sorts of culinary moments. I've heard chefs brag about the food from their particular region of the country, but I've never seen the sort of passion that pours forth when an Alaska chef starts talking about the state's world-class seafood. From the fat scallops of Kodiak Island to the prized salmon from the Copper River to the crisp oysters of Prince William Sound, Alaska's professional chefs have a stunning set of raw ingredients to chose from—and all at only a fraction of what it might cost in the Lower 48.

Alaska has other culinary gifts, too. Nearly round-the-clock daylight in the summer produces an abundance of herbs, greens, and other vegetables, including cabbages so big a single one might easily keep a restaurant in cole slaw for weeks. In the state's interior, morel mushrooms can grow as big as your hand. Unusual game meats, such as caribou and moose, present themselves in the fall and winter. In the hands of skilled Alaska chefs, such natural bounty becomes the sophisticated, regional food of the North. Any serious eater who has visited Alaska leaves pleasantly surprised by the quality of the cuisine served in both city restaurants and remote fishing lodges.

The chefs who venture to Alaska are as resourceful—and sometimes as quirky—as many of the rest of the state's 650,000 residents. Like the prospectors of the Klondike Gold Rush, they move north for adventure and opportunity and find it in kitchens from Juneau to Barrow. Some of the cooks learned their craft cooking meat and potatoes for the people who built the Alaska oil pipeline. Others earned their chops in remote hunting lodges. Some have more sophisticated roots, heading north after graduating from American culinary school or apprenticeships in European kitchens.

No matter what their background, Alaska chefs have to be creative in a state where weather, geography, and even the palate of the population can pose a serious challenge in the kitchen. Imagine having to figure out how to secure fresh arugula or raspberries during a cold snap that sends the temperature down to 40 below zero. Or the dedication it takes to get up at 3 a.m. to bid for the best black truffles from France.

The evolution of Alaska's food scene has been swift. The band of European-trained chefs who moved north just after Alaska achieved statehood in 1959 set the foundation. The skills of chefs who worked in oil pipeline camps and on fishing ships grew along with the state in the 1970s. In the 1980s, when the state began to boom with more money from oil and tourism, Alaska's best chefs cooked in hotels and lodges and on cruise ships. And when the American food revolution, with its emphasis on regional ingredients, took hold in the 1990s, Alaska's best chefs began opening their own restaurants and elevating the food served in remote lodges.

You'll find the result of that evolution in this book, which is the first to gather in one place the best recipes Alaska's best chefs have to offer. Taken as a whole, the recipes reflect a new style of Alaska cooking. They range from simple instructions for a perfect piece of alder-roasted fish to more challenging methods for fusion-influenced vegan main dishes. You'll find elegant appetizers like ricotta Dungeness crab cakes and vodka-cured gravlax and comforting desserts like warm berry crisp with birch syrup and, of course, baked Alaska.

Each recipe was tested by Glenn Denkler, a former hotshot chef from Anchorage who is now one of the state's most respected culinary instructors. Denkler can't stand a recipe that doesn't work, so you can trust that his translations of the chefs' recipes for the home cook are accurate.

With a collection like this, only a handful of the state's chefs could be included. I regret I could not highlight the work of more people, because there are plenty of professionals across the state turning out food as good as the dishes contained in these pages. Nonetheless, I hope you find this book to be a workable, honest reflection of the cooking styles and personalities of the women and men who cook in the kitchens of the Last Frontier.

—*Kim Severson*

The Chefs

Jack Amon

Jack Amon claims he brought the sun-dried tomato to Alaska, and it may well be true. A self-taught, self-assured chef with Greek blood, Amon has led the Marx Bros. Cafe kitchen for more than twenty years. The little restaurant in an old house in downtown Anchorage boasts an 11,000-bottle wine cellar. It is the place many Alaskans go to celebrate new romances, new babies, and other life passages, including the coming of spring—an event worthy of a party in Alaska. The restaurant's reputation rests on Caesar salads made tableside, innovative use of products from Alaska's oceans and forests, and fusion-influenced dishes like macadamia nut–crusted halibut with Thai coconut curry. Amon grows a kitchen garden during the short, intense Alaska summer and takes his influence from the simple, straightforward approach of restaurants like Alice Waters's Chez Panisse in Berkeley, California.

Amon headed north in 1974 to work on the Trans-Alaska Pipeline. Although he had little kitchen experience, Amon ended up cooking in roughneck camps and eventually talked his way into the best hotel kitchen in the state. In 1979, he opened the Marx Bros. Cafe with wine guru Van Hale and partner Ken Brown. Alaska had seen nothing like it. At the time, the notion of fine dining in Alaska was cherries jubilee and lobster tails. Amon recalls having to get up at 3 A.M. to order fresh arugula and strawberries from the Los Angeles produce markets. "Our goal was a restaurant that would rival any in the Pacific Northwest. We wanted to put Anchorage on the culinary map," he says. "Alaska has come a long way food-wise since then, but there's still plenty of room for innovation."

JoAnn Asher

JoAnn Asher believes that the best dining experiences are born from collaboration. That's why, on any given day, the menu at her stylish Sacks Cafe in downtown Anchorage will be built from several people's recipes—some of which she chose to include in this book. "You have to rely on other people to survive in Alaska. That's the approach we take in the kitchen," she says.

Asher, a world traveler and former waitress, drove from the San Francisco Bay Area to Alaska in an overstuffed Toyota in 1981. She met her former partner, Margie Brown, while they both worked at the Marx

Bros. Cafe. At the time it was the hottest restaurant in Alaska. The pair decided to open Sacks in a little space downtown near the Anchorage Performing Arts Center in 1983. They began cooking a sort of upscale American regional food with Asian and Mediterranean twists and, of course, much of it centered on seafood. They recently moved to a sleek, 84-seat space a few blocks away from their original location. "People say it looks like what you'd find in San Francisco or even New York. I say why can't we have this in Alaska?" Asher says. The menu continues to expand, including dishes as elevated as Asian five-spice scallops with carrot-ginger coconut cream and as simple but creative as a sirloin burger with chipotle mayonnaise on a baguette. "Everyone calls our food New American," Asher says, "but it's really New Alaskan."

Kirsten Dixon

Kirsten Dixon is sort of the Martha Stewart of the North. And why not? She is arguably the best-known Alaska cook, and her food reflects both her relationship with the land that surrounds her three wilderness lodges and her sophisticated sensibility. Dixon was the first to lead a group of Alaska chefs to New York to cook at the prestigious James Beard House and has taken her comfortable Alaska-style cooking to Los Angeles and London. You'll need to take a plane to any of the three lodges that make up her Within the Wild Adventure Company; none are accessible by road. They include Winterlake Lodge, 198 trail miles northwest of Anchorage along Alaska's historic Iditarod Trail, and Redoubt Bay Lodge at Lake Clark Pass. The anchor is Riversong Lodge, about an hour's flight by floatplane northwest from Anchorage. The lodge has attracted everyone from French winemakers to American recording stars.

Dixon and her husband, Carl, left the medical profession to open Riversong in 1983. Dixon picked up many of her cooking skills from a parade of visiting chefs and foodies who teach classes at her lodges or work the summers there. For Dixon, the challenge of cooking in Alaska has always been the remoteness of her kitchens. Generators make walk-in temperatures uneven. Delicate foods need to be hand-carried and delivered by floatplane or ski plane. And although she travels as much as she can, Dixon often feels isolated from the larger food community. "Another challenge is the wildlife. We have bears that get into our kitchen, rip open the root cellar, break into freezers, and haul trash out of our dump area," she says. "We have to constantly manage that situation at all three of my lodges." But the challenges are nothing when weighed against the life she has made with her husband and two daughters. "We live in such a beautiful place, it makes up for any challenges we might face."

Jens Hansen

Jens Hansen might well be called the father of new Alaska cooking. At one time or another, many of Alaska's best chefs have spent time in his kitchen or as members of the Alaska chefs' association he helped start. Hansen is a wild Dane with a deep passion for food and wine and something of a rogue's reputation in a state full of them.

Seeking adventure, Hansen came to Alaska in 1968 after formal training in Copenhagen and Paris. He got his feet wet in a hotel kitchen and then headed to the North Slope to cook for the people building the Alaska pipeline. But Hansen really hit his stride when he ran the Crow's Nest atop the Hotel Captain Cook in Anchorage during the wild, free-spending oil boom days in the late 1970s and early 1980s. During those years, Hansen and a handful of other classically trained Europeans like Hans Kruger had a profound impact on Alaska's professional kitchens. They demanded better produce from their purveyors and taught many old sourdoughs the delights of classic sauces and good wine. "When I came here there were only potatoes and cabbages. Really. There was not fresh meat. Nothing," he says. "Everybody thought I was nuts for my little tantrums over the lack of fresh vegetables or the quality of meat." In 1988, he opened his namesake restaurant, Jens' Restaurant and Bodega, in a strip mall in the middle of Anchorage. Pepper steaks, perfect plates of sautéed fish, and traditional Danish dishes give way later in the evening to glasses of wine and singing in the bar. Every winter, he takes off for a month, flying to exotic locales like South Africa, New Zealand, and Belize. "You've got to travel, man," he says. "Otherwise it would be the same eight guys all copying each other."

Jennifer Jolis

Jennifer Jolis immersed herself deep in Alaska's wild country before she changed the dining landscape in Fairbanks, a city of 70,000 that freezes in September and stays well below zero for several months. Her first taste of the state came in 1966 when she volunteered for the VISTA program, landing in a small Native village just north of the Arctic Circle. She was cooking on a Coleman stove and baking in a makeshift oven when she received an ill-timed present from her grandmother: a copy of Julia Child's *Mastering the Art of French Cooking*.

She did not attempt to cook professionally until 1980 when, after taking some cooking classes in New York, she started making desserts for a restaurant in Fairbanks. That job led to catering, which led to A Moveable Feast, a relaxed restaurant that served fresh soups, salads, and sandwiches. Alaska's economic crash in the mid-1980s, coupled with the Exxon *Valdez* oil spill ("I went through 21 dishwashers in 22 days. Everyone headed south to work on the cleanup," she says), spelled the end of the restaurant. She continued to cook around the state at places as far-flung as the Aleutian Islands, learning more about the state's indigenous ingredients. In 1996, she started Jennifer's in Fairbanks, a white-tablecloth restaurant that brought big-city techniques, savory custards, white truffle oil, and organic greens to the city's restaurant scene. She recently sold the restaurant to spend time with sick friends and to soothe a chef's form of carpal tunnel syndrome, but she still cooks for fund-raising events and friends. And she hasn't forgotten the lessons from her early days in Alaska, among them the fact that moosehead soup and a good pot-au-feu have a lot in common: "Both can be very good if well made."

Farrokh Larijani

Farrokh Larijani grew up in Tehran, Iran, watching his father cook. When he was fourteen, his family moved to Seattle and he got his first restaurant job: washing dishes in a steak house. He was hooked, eventually graduating from Portland's Western Culinary Institute. He was working for a chain of high-end restaurants in Seattle when the company offered to send him to one of two overseas properties. The choice: Alaska or Hawaii. "I took one look at my wife and she said, 'Let's give it a shot.'" It was the right call.

In 1996, two years after he arrived, Larijani was tapped to run the Glacier BrewHouse, Anchorage's sexy entry in the Northwest brewpub trend. With a wood-burning oven, an open-flame grill, and a rotisserie, Larijani built a strong menu featuring dishes like halibut with roasted corn salsa, thin-crusted pizzas with local wild mushrooms, and spit-roasted pork loin chops with garlic-infused mashed potatoes. His simple but sophisticated approach in the kitchen also helped define Orso, an Italian sister restaurant to the BrewHouse that opened next door in the summer of 2000. When he's not in one of the restaurants, you can find Larijani at a soccer game, raising scholarship money for culinary students, or mentoring a young cook.

Larijani says the best thing about cooking in Alaska is the wild fish, which is the envy of his chef friends in the Lower 48. But they don't envy how difficult it is to get good-quality seasonal produce, especially in the middle of a six-month-long winter. "You just have to bite the bullet sometimes" he says. "But that's the fun of it—dealing with the elements." Travel is the key for chefs in Alaska, he adds. "The bottom line is you've got to get out of the state to see what's hot and what's not."

David and JoAnn Lesh

Dave Lesh cooks in Gustavus, a tiny town clinging to the edge of Glacier Bay National Park in Southeast Alaska. The area was home for generations to Tlingit Indians, who built camps and smoked salmon there. White settlers and, later, back-to-nature hippies followed, helping to carve Gustavus's modern-day character. What's surprising is that for a town of four hundred in an isolated stretch of Alaska wilderness, Gustavus has some extraordinary food. A hungry traveler might choose from pan-Asian and classic European dishes at the nearby Glacier Bay Country Inn or the homey, comforting food of the Gustavus Inn that Lesh and his wife, JoAnn, run.

Lesh's mother and father, Sally and Jack, homesteaded the site along the Salmon River almost 30 years ago. Sally was considered a fine cook, and her food drew travelers who had no other reason to head to Gustavus except to stay at the inn. Today, Lesh keeps the homespun tradition going but frequently adds new twists, whether it's a better sourdough pancake or a new method to prepare salmon. Dishes might include local morel mushrooms, fresh raspberries, and just-caught crab or sablefish. But no matter how tony food at the Gustavus Inn gets, visitors can always order Halibut Caddy Ganty, a rich mix of halibut, onions, sour cream, and mayonnaise that originated in Pelican, Alaska, and was made popular at the Gustavus Inn. The dish, often called Halibut Olympia, is now ubiquitous on menus all over the state. "What matters to people who eat here is that the food is honest and that it shows the best of what we've got growing around here," Lesh says.

Al Levinsohn

Al Levinsohn has the enviable task of making the food at the Alyeska Resort, the finest hotel property in the state, as beautiful as the mountains and ocean that surround it. The challenge doesn't faze Levinsohn, who has cooked everywhere from the Regal Hotel in Hong Kong to the James Beard House in New York City. That's not to say Levinsohn didn't have some adjusting to do when he moved north in 1984 to work at the Crow's Nest in the Hotel Captain Cook. Although the California-born chef had been coming to Alaska to visit since he was a child, he didn't realize the state's laid-back attitude would extend to one of the best kitchens in Anchorage. "I came from a strict background," Levinsohn says. "I had to learn that Alaskans have a certain regimen that wasn't like any other professional kitchen I'd been in." It didn't take him long to settle in. After that first job he went on to run the kitchens in the Regal Alaskan Hotel and opened the well-appointed Alyeska Prince Hotel in the ski resort 40 miles south of Anchorage. After a short stint as the opening chef for the Glacier BrewHouse, he returned to the Alyeska Resort as executive chef. The job involves overseeing five restaurants, including a traditional teppanyaki grill and the innovative Seven Glaciers at the top of Mount Alyeska, accessible only by a 60-passenger tram. There, dishes might include pepper-crusted rack of venison, duck sausage on polenta with black truffle, and Alaska seafood dishes like mussel chowder.

The challenges of cooking in Alaska have changed, he says. For one thing, much better produce is available. "It was rough in the early 1980s—you'd get cases of yellowed, flowered broccoli and that was it. Take it or leave it." Now availability is better and so is the state's collective palate. That is both good and bad. "Used to be you could blow people away pretty easily with new and different stuff they'd never seen," he says. "Now, it takes more work to really wow people."

Mark Linden

Mark Linden, former executive chef at the Anchorage Hilton Hotel, is probably the most unassuming and possibly the hardest-working chef in Alaska. You'd never know from his easygoing approach to life that he was the chef picked to coordinate a barbecue in a hangar for 1,500 people when the Anchorage airport was renamed after Senator Ted Stevens. Or that he is one of two Alaska men ever to try for the grueling and exclusive American Culinary Federation Master Chef certification. Or that for years he has been a quiet leader of Alaska's chef community, helping with scholarships and mentoring young cooks.

Linden, a graduate of the Culinary Institute of America, traveled to Alaska in 1982 chasing pipeline money. That didn't last long, and he ended up at the Sheraton Anchorage Hotel. Soon after, he arrived in the kitchen at the Anchorage Hilton, Alaska's largest hotel. In the late 1970s and early 1980s, after the state got rich with oil money, people looking for sophisticated, well-prepared food headed to the restaurants in Anchorage's biggest hotels, like the Top of the World at the Hilton.

Although most of the cutting-edge cooking in Alaska is now being done in smaller restaurants and a handful of exclusive lodges, hotels still play a key role in defining Alaska's cuisine, especially to some of the one million tourists who arrive in Alaska each summer. After a long run with the Hilton, Linden left the hotel to help chef Scott Evers run Glacial Reflections Fine Catering in Anchorage. Linden says people wrongly see Alaska as isolated. "Anchorage has access to the world. We can get whatever we want in a day," he says. "And we chefs are just as talented and creative as people outside. We've got the world at our fingertips."

Sean Maryott

Sean Maryott revolutionized food in Homer, a town of 5,000 literally at the end of the road on Alaska's Highway 1. Almost every plate of decent pasta and every imaginative menu twist can be traced back somehow to this Arizona native who started his career as a cook at a golf course country club. Maryott, who never had a formal culinary education, spends summers surprising tourists with innovative food at the Homestead Restaurant, a lovely log roadhouse about eight miles outside of Homer. The menu reflects the bounty of Kachemak Bay and greens grown by local farmers. In the winter, locals who have had their fill of halibut and salmon stop by and settle into heartier plates of smoked or roasted meats like lamb or beef. Dishes out of Maryott's kitchen might get Asian spicing, a Southwest kick, or some texture and verve from an exotic fruit. All are built with scratch stocks and sauces. "For me, everything is flavor. I like food that has a little juiciness to it," Maryott says.

Like many who call Homer home, Maryott came north to work on a fishing boat for a summer in the 1980s. His first high-profile cooking job came when he took over as chef at the Land's End Resort. A few years later, he talked his then-wife and two other people from the hotel into joining him to open Café Cups, a restaurant that soon became synonymous with hip food in Homer. Several Cups veterans have gone on to open their own restaurants, spreading the sort of in-tune, creative approach to food that Maryott embodies. Maryott has since sold Cups, and focuses exclusively on The Homestead, which he opened in 1983. He mentors talented college students who come north for the summer, much as he did. And he continues to fight to get top-drawer produce and meats into Homer, which sometimes gets the dregs since it is truly at the end of the line. "I like to think I started a new wave of attitude toward food in Homer," he says.

Kirk McLean

Kirk McLean is a relative newcomer to the Alaska food scene, but he is making a name for himself with fresh techniques and thoughtful use of ingredients. Of course, it doesn't hurt that in 1999 he took over the kitchen of one of Alaska's best-known eating establishments, the Fiddlehead Restaurant and Bakery in Juneau. Since its inception more than two decades ago, the Fiddlehead has been a comfortable place that showed off the best of Alaska's woodlands and waterways. It can hold its own against restaurants in the Lower 48, and two of its former chefs have run the state governor's kitchen. Deborah Marshall, who had nurtured the Fiddlehead since 1978, recently sold it, and the new owners worked with McLean to update the menu. The more formal upstairs dining room, called the Fireweed Room, now draws its influence from Tuscany. The main restaurant downstairs, long a vegetarian's delight and a sure bet for hearty breakfasts, boasts a few more meat dishes.

McLean, who was raised in the San Francisco Bay Area, spent fifteen years cooking in California's Sonoma Valley, traveling to Alaska for a month each summer. The contrast between the sorts of raw ingredients available in Alaska compared with Northern California was startling at first. But McLean quickly learned to use the best local purveyors, supplemented by airfreight orders from Hawaii and the Lower 48. And to keep up on trends back in his beloved California, he turns to the World Wide Web. "I can always find something for inspiration on the Net," he says.

Jens Nannestad

Jens Nannestad's food is upscale but accessible, innovative but not over the top. The combination makes his Anchorage restaurant, Southside Bistro, one of the gems of Alaska dining. "We have quite a sophisticated clientele up here, but we have to realize we're in Alaska and not get too 'Aqua' on them," he says, referring to the four-star San Francisco restaurant. It's no surprise that Nannestad would reference the Bay Area restaurant scene—for a decade he traveled between Alaska and Northern California before putting down roots up north in the mid-1990s. He started his career in Austria, as an apprentice for a demanding chef, and later graduated from the California Culinary Academy.

Nannestad landed in Alaska in 1985 and worked in the Hotel Captain Cook's top restaurant, the Crow's Nest. The young immigrant got his green card and headed back to the Bay Area. He took a job as a chef on a cruise ship and met his wife and business partner, Megan. They settled in

Alaska. After a couple of jobs in other people's kitchens, Nannestad opened Southside Bistro in 1995. His biggest challenge remains finding talent, particularly cooks with a formal culinary education. He feels lucky to have found his chef de cuisine, Alaska-born Elizabeth King, and even includes some of her recipes in this book. Like most professional chefs in Alaska, Nannestad has no plans to leave: "There's still some fun left in it here. It's not so competitive, so it's still entertaining."

A Note about the Recipes

from Chef Glenn Denkler

Recipes are interesting phenomena. By themselves, many recipes have probably intimidated or turned off oodles of potential cooks. What a shame! Let me attempt to demystify the process.

The culinary profession is divided into two groups of folks, bakers and cooks. Cooks use recipes as a guideline in preparing food. Professional bakers don't call recipes "recipes"; they call them formulas. The ingredients in formulas react with each other in an exact scientific way, so measurements must be precise. On the other hand, cooks focus more on a recipe as a general guideline that they can be flexible with.

The point is that in cooking, flavors are not static. Two tomatoes from the same bin may have different tastes. Fresh basil purchased from one store may be more intense than a bunch from another. A recipe should be considered a starting point. A cook must learn to taste and not be a slave to a recipe. Food must be continually tasted and flavors adjusted during the cooking process. The more a cook tastes, the better the cook.

So, treat these recipes with respect; respect the talent of the cooks who came up with the ideas, but have fun. If you don't like an ingredient or amount, be bold and experiment. If you can't get wild Alaska salmon or Kodiak scallops, find the best seafood you can, given the state of your local fish market. Cultivated mushrooms can substitute for wild ones in a pinch. Asparagus can work in place of fiddleheads, and so on. (Of course, be more careful with the desserts.) Let your heart and your taste buds rule.

A Couple of Technical Points and Tips

- Temperatures are in Fahrenheit.
- Eggs are large.
- Buy the best products you can afford. You will be rewarded.
- Read the recipe completely through; gather all the ingredients, cooking pans, and utensils; and preheat the oven if necessary before beginning to cook.

Appetizers

Alaskan Smoked Salmon Bruschetta

Al Levinsohn, Alyeska Resort

Smoked salmon is everywhere in Alaska. Many people have home smokers or bring their summer's catch to professional meat and fish processors for smoking or for lox. This dish is a quick starter that can be thrown together if friends drop by. Other smoked fish may be substituted.

½ cup diced (¼ inch) ripe tomatoes
¼ cup thinly sliced fresh basil
2 tablespoons feta
¼ cup flaked smoked Alaska king salmon
12 slices baguette, cut on the bias ½ inch thick
¼ cup extra virgin olive oil

- Preheat the oven to 400°F.

- Combine the tomatoes, basil, feta, and salmon in a small bowl. Set aside.

- Brush each slice of bread on both sides with olive oil. Place the slices of bread on a cookie sheet and toast in the oven until well browned and crisp. Remove from the oven and let cool to room temperature.

- Top each slice of toast with an equal amount of the salmon mixture.

Serves four

Pan-Seared Alaska Oysters with Fennel and Leeks

Kirsten Dixon, Winterlake Lodge

Because the water in Alaska is so cold, oysters don't reproduce. That makes for crisp, firm oysters year-round. The trade-off, however, is that the handful of professional oyster growers have to import Pacific oyster spat from Washington.

This oyster appetizer has become a popular first course at Winterlake Lodge. Dixon serves it in some variation all year long. She adds trimmed pieces of fennel to the reducing cream for flavor. Sometimes she deep-fries the oysters with a panko (Japanese bread crumb) crust. She likes to use deep-fried basil as a garnish, as well.

> 24 fresh Alaska oysters
> 2 cups heavy cream
> 1 medium fennel bulb, trimmed and quartered
> 1 tablespoon butter
> 2 small leeks, trimmed and halved
> 2 tablespoons grapeseed oil
> 24 white pearl onions, peeled and blanched
> Ground sea salt and ground white pepper

- Shuck the oysters, reserving their liquor. Strain the liquor through rinsed cheesecloth and pour into a medium saucepan. Add the cream. Bring the cream and liquor mixture just to a simmer, then reduce the heat to low, and reduce the sauce slowly by half.

- In a medium sauté pan over medium heat, fry the fennel in butter until tender. Reduce the heat to low and add the leeks. Cover and cook until soft. Remove fennel and leeks and keep warm.

- Refresh the onions in a saucepan of simmering water for 1 minute.

- Add the grapeseed oil to the sauté pan and increase the heat to medium-high. Pan-sear oysters for about 1 minute on each side.

- Pour about ¼ cup of the reduced cream and oyster liquor sauce onto warmed plates. Place 6 oysters on each plate. Add leek, 1 fennel quarter, and 6 pearl onions. Season with salt and pepper to taste.

  Serves four

Shrimp Cakes with Cilantro Sauce and Maui Onion Salad

Mark Linden, Glacial Reflections Catering

This is a nice alternative to crab cakes that takes advantage of sweet Maui onions.

SHRIMP MIXTURE

1 pound Alaska spot or side-striped shrimp, peeled, deveined, poached, and rough chopped

½ teaspoon grated fresh ginger

½ cup mayonnaise

1 egg

1 pinch cayenne

1 teaspoon fresh lime juice

2 tablespoons chopped cilantro

½ teaspoon Tabasco

1 teaspoon heavy cream

½ cup panko (Japanese bread crumbs, available in Asian markets and some supermarkets)

2 green onions, sliced thin

½ teaspoon soy sauce

1 teaspoon Dijon mustard

½ teaspoon Old Bay Seasoning

Salt and pepper

BREADING

2 cups flour

4 eggs, beaten

3 cups panko

½ cup olive oil

GARNISH

Cilantro Sauce (page 6)

Maui Onion Salad (page 7)

■ For the shrimp mixture, gently combine all ingredients in a large bowl. Make a small patty and fry it in 1 tablespoon of olive oil until cooked through. Taste it for seasoning and adjust with salt and pepper.

- Cover a baking tray that will fit into the freezer with plastic wrap. Divide the shrimp mixture into 8 balls, then shape them into patties. Place the patties on the prepared baking tray and freeze for 1 hour. This will make them easier to handle while breading and cooking.

- To bread the shrimp, set out 3 shallow bowls. Place the 2 cups of flour in the first, the beaten eggs in the second, and the panko in the third. Remove the patties from the freezer. One at a time, dredge the patties in the flour and shake off excess, dip into the eggs, and press both sides into the panko.

- Heat the 1/2 cup olive oil in a heavy skillet over medium heat and pan-fry the patties on both sides until golden brown. Remove and drain on paper towels. Keep warm.

- Serve with cilantro sauce and garnish with Maui onion salad.

    Serves four

Cilantro Sauce

    1 cup mayonnaise
    2 tablespoons chopped cilantro
    1 1/2 teaspoons grated fresh ginger
    2 tablespoons rice wine vinegar
    1 1/2 teaspoons fresh lemon juice
    2 tablespoons minced green pepper
    1 green onion, sliced thin
    Salt and freshly ground pepper to taste

- Combine all ingredients and refrigerate.

    Makes 1 1/2 cups

Maui Onion Salad

 2 tablespoons olive oil
 3 tablespoons minced pancetta
 ¼ teaspoon minced garlic
 1 teaspoon minced shallots
 2 teaspoons balsamic vinegar
 6 leaves basil, cut into thin strips
 2 small Maui onions, cut into thin strips

■ In a heavy sauté pan, heat the olive oil over medium heat until it shimmers. Add the pancetta and cook until it is crisp. Remove and set aside. Add the garlic and shallots, cook for 30 seconds, add the vinegar, and cook until it simmers. Remove the mixture from the pan and let cool. Add the bacon, basil, and onions to the cooled mixture and stir to combine. Hold at room temperature until ready to use.

 Serves four

Cilantro-Cured Salmon with Avocado Pico de Gallo

Kirk McLean, Fiddlehead Restaurant and Bakery

Like the rest of America, Alaska's chefs have been influenced by the cooking styles of Mexico and Latin America. This dish combines Alaska's most identifiable food—salmon—with the flavor of Mexico. It takes a few days of refrigerator time, but the basic preparation is simple. The salsa is an unusual addition.

> 1 fillet (4 pounds) fresh salmon, skinless, trimmed, bones removed
> 2 cups sugar
> 2 cups kosher salt
> 2 bunches of cilantro
> Avocado Pico de Gallo (page 9)

- Coat one side of the salmon with half of the sugar, then half of the salt. Rinse the cilantro well and roughly chop.

- Place a layer of heavy-duty plastic wrap long enough to wrap back over the top of the salmon when finished in a shallow pan large enough to hold the salmon.

- Spread out half of the cilantro in the shape of the fillet on the plastic wrap. Place the coated side of salmon down on top of the cilantro. Repeat the coating procedure on the exposed side of the salmon, beginning with sugar, then salt, then cilantro. Fold the excess plastic wrap over the exposed salmon. Place another pan on top of the fillet. Set heavy cans on the pan to weigh down the salmon. Place the pan on the bottom rack of the refrigerator. Refrigerate for 48 to 72 hours, removing excess liquid periodically.

- Unwrap the salmon, rinse, and pat dry. Slice the salmon very thin, arrange on a platter and garnish with avocado pico de gallo.

> Serves eight

Avocado Pico de Gallo

2 ripe Hass avocados, peeled, pitted, and diced
1 tablespoon fresh lime juice
1 ripe tomato, cored and diced
1 small red onion, finely diced
1 tablespoon minced garlic
¼ cup chopped cilantro
Salt and ground black pepper

- Combine avocados and lime juice in a bowl. Gently blend in the tomato, red onion, garlic, and cilantro. Season with salt and pepper to taste.

Makes 3 cups

Deviled Crab Cakes with Red Chile Mayonnaise

Jack Amon, Marx Bros. Cafe

Crab is plentiful during the fall and winter. Alaskans eat compact, meaty Dungeness from Southeast and impossibly big King crab from the Bering Sea off the western edge of the state. These crab cakes have long been a favorite at the Marx Bros. Cafe. The mayonnaise is just spicy enough to give the crab cakes a kick without overpowering them.

1 tablespoon butter
2 teaspoons minced onion
¼ teaspoon minced garlic
1 tablespoon minced red pepper
1 tablespoon minced yellow pepper
4 teaspoons flour
⅓ cup heavy cream
1 teaspoon dry mustard
2 teaspoons prepared mustard
2 teaspoons mixed herbs, such as basil, parsley, and/or chives
¼ teaspoon cayenne
Dash of Tabasco
1 egg yolk
10 ounces Dungeness crabmeat, picked over, rinsed if salted
1 teaspoon fresh lemon juice
1¼ cups fresh bread crumbs
1 cup milk
1 egg
Clarified Butter, for frying (page 205)
Romaine lettuce, thinly sliced
Red Chile Mayonnaise (page 11)

■ Melt the butter in a skillet. Add the onion, garlic, and peppers. Cook over low heat 2 to 3 minutes. Add the flour and stir until well incorporated. Cook 2 to 3 minutes more, but do not allow it to brown. Gradually add the cream and stir until thickened. Add the dry and prepared mustards, herbs, cayenne, and Tabasco, mixing well. Stir in the egg yolk. Quickly add the crabmeat, lemon juice, and ¼ cup of the bread crumbs, stirring until well blended. Remove from the heat and refrigerate for 4 hours or overnight.

- Divide the chilled mixture into 12 equal portions. Shape each one carefully into an oval. Whip the milk and egg together. Dip the crab ovals into the egg-milk mixture, then into the remaining 1 cup bread crumbs.

- Fry the crab ovals in clarified butter until golden brown on each side. Drain on paper towels. Serve three per person on a bed of thinly sliced Romaine lettuce with a dollop of red chile mayonnaise.

  Serves four

Red Chile Mayonnaise

   1 teaspoon *sambal oelek* (Thai chile sauce, available at Asian markets)
   3 cloves garlic
   4 tablespoons fresh lime juice
   2 tablespoons prepared mustard
   2 eggs
   1 cup olive oil
   1 cup vegetable oil
   Salt and pepper

- Combine the *sambal oelek* with the garlic and lime juice in a food processor. Add the mustard and eggs. Process until well mixed. With the processor running, add a fourth of the oil, 1 tablespoon at a time. With the processor still running, add the remainder of the oil in a thin, steady stream. Adjust the seasoning with salt and pepper to taste.

  Makes 2½ cups

Gorgonzola Soufflé

Jennifer Jolis, Jennifer's

In Fairbanks, where the temperature is below zero for weeks on end and the sun doesn't shine for months, a little sophistication is in order. This creation is an elegant soufflé that can work as a light supper or luncheon dish. Serve it with good bread and a green salad.

> 2 teaspoons plus 3 tablespoons butter
> 4 tablespoons flour
> ¾ cup whole milk
> 3½ ounces Gorgonzola
> 2 egg yolks
> Pinch of ground nutmeg
> Salt and pepper
> 3 egg whites

- Preheat the oven to 400°F.

- Butter four 4-ounce ramekins with 2 teaspoons butter. Flour the buttered ramekins with 1 tablespoon of the flour. Pour out the excess.

- Melt the remaining 3 tablespoons butter in saucepan over low heat. When melted, whisk in the remaining 3 tablespoons flour. Continue cooking over low heat, stirring constantly with a wooden spoon, until a nutty aroma develops, and watching that the mixture does not brown, about 5 minutes.

- In a separate pan, heat the milk until small bubbles form around the edges.

- Remove the flour-butter mixture from the heat, add the hot milk and let sit for 1 minute, then whisk well. Return to the heat, stirring constantly with the wooden spoon, until the mixture begins to simmer. Adjust the heat to maintain a simmer and cook for 5 minutes. Remove from the heat and stir in the cheese.

- Whisk the yolks in a bowl, then slowly add ¼ cup of the milk mixture to the yolks, whisking constantly. Whisk the yolk mixture into the remaining milk mixture. Add the nutmeg and salt and pepper to taste.

- With a clean whip, whisk the egg whites to the soft peak stage. Stir a fourth of the whites into the yolk mixture, then fold in the remaining whites. Pour into the prepared ramekins.

- Place the ramekins in a baking tray at least 1 inch deep. Pour hot water around the ramekins until the water level is halfway up the side of the ramekins.

- Bake for about 16 minutes, or until the soufflés have risen and are golden on top. Serve right away.

Serves four

Forest Mushroom Tarts

Kirsten Dixon, Riversong Lodge

Eating from the land matters to many Alaskans, even if it is a just few wild berries or one of the easily identifiable edible mushrooms that grow in many parts of the state. Morels pop up in the spring and King boletes, or porcinis, grow all summer and into early fall.

For these tarts, blanch the mushrooms so that they don't release moisture and make the crusts soggy.

> ½ cup heavy cream
> 1 tablespoon plus 1 teaspoon plus 2 teaspoons butter
> 1 large leek, cleaned, trimmed, and sliced
> Salt and freshly ground black pepper
> 1 pound porcini or other wild mushrooms, stems removed and discarded
> Four 5-inch-square sheets of puff pastry
> 4 teaspoons fresh thyme
> 1 clove garlic, minced
> 2 tablespoons grapeseed oil

- Preheat the oven to 400°F.

- In a medium pot, bring to a boil enough water to cover the mushrooms.

- At the same time, pour the cream into a saucepan and bring to a very gentle simmer.

- Melt 1 tablespoon of butter in a medium sauté pan over medium heat and add the leek. Reduce the heat to low, cover, and cook just until soft, 6 to 8 minutes. Add the leeks to the cream and simmer over medium heat until the cream reduces by half and glazes the leeks. Season with salt and pepper to taste.

- Cook the mushrooms in the boiling water for 3 minutes, drain, and rinse. Heat a small sauté pan over medium heat. Add 1 teaspoon of butter. Add the mushrooms and cook until all the moisture is evaporated. Set aside.

- Lay out the puff pastry sheets on a floured work surface, and sprinkle with thyme and pepper. Use a rolling pin to press the thyme and pepper into the dough and to stretch out the sheets by ½ inch. Cut each sheet into a 4-inch circle. Prick the pastry all over with the tines of a fork. Place the sheets on a jelly-roll pan lined with parchment paper. Brush the tops of the circles with the remaining 2 teaspoons butter.

- Spread a fourth of the leek-cream mixture on each circle, leaving a 1-inch border. Layer the mushrooms on top of the leeks. Combine the garlic and grapeseed oil. Brush half of this mixture over the tarts.

- Bake the tarts until golden brown, checking after 10 minutes. Remove from the oven and brush with remaining garlic-oil mixture. Serve right away.

Serves four

Into the Forest

On the way home from a three-day hike through Denali National Park, we stopped to stretch our legs. There, just a few yards from the car, was the largest hedgehog mushroom I had ever seen. We walked a little deeper into the woods and patches of the tan mushrooms blanketed the forest floor. We dropped to our knees and gathered as many as we could carry home. The next night, I made a big pot of hedgehog soup with plenty of cream and sherry.

Foraging for mushrooms and other forest edibles is common practice all over Alaska. In the interior, forest fires mark the land and make prime territory for spring's elusive morel mushroom. In the fall, king boletes, called cèpes in France and porcini in Italy, grow readily. A few days foraging in the fall and a good supply can be dried for winter.

But mushrooms aren't the only gems in Alaska's forest. In the southeast, the tips of young spruce are gathered to make beer and jam. Young, tightly coiled ostrich fern fronds are a wonderful spring treat. Called fiddleheads, they resemble the curved end of a violin. When the shoots have just pushed their way through the earth, they are perfect for sautéing in nothing but butter and a sprinkle of salt. They taste grassy and green, like asparagus.

Berries of all sorts are the food of high summer, and have long played an important part in the diets of Alaska Natives. Black and red currants, raspberries, cranberries, blackberries, and a host of other berries grow throughout Alaska. Blueberries are a particular pleasure, and they end up in a year-round parade of jams, jellies, and pancakes. The careful cook makes sure several containers are put in the freezer, preserving the abundance of summer to use during the long winter.

Fireweed makes for sweet honey, and rose hips can be dried and boiled into tea or made into jam. Even snow sweetened with a little birch syrup can be a delightful way to enjoy a taste of Alaska wilderness in the middle of winter.

Orso Clams

Farrokh Larijani, Orso

Many pristine beaches in Southcentral and Southeast Alaska hold round butter clams and the more delicate-shelled and meaty razor clams. This is a very simple way to prepare fresh clams and reflects a style of cooking at Orso, one of Larijani's restaurants. If you ever go clamming and plan ahead, this is an item that you can fix right on the open fire on the beach. Sit back and enjoy the scenery.

½ cup olive oil
½ cup fennel strips (2 inches)
½ cup yellow onion strips (2 inches)
1½ teaspoons chopped garlic
½ teaspoon crushed red pepper
1 cup Shellfish Stock (page 201)
1 cup dry vermouth
1 lemon, peeled, seeded, and chopped
3 tablespoons chopped basil
1 tablespoon chopped fresh thyme
1 cup Roasted Roma Tomatoes (page 190)
1 teaspoon fennel seeds
½ teaspoon salt
Pinch of ground black pepper
4 pounds Manila clams, scrubbed
¼ cup Lemon Herb Butter (page 193)
8 Polenta Croutons (page 172)
3 tablespoons chopped Italian parsley

- Heat the olive oil in a large pot over medium-high heat until it shimmers. Add the fennel and onions and cook, stirring until soft. Add the garlic and red pepper and cook for 30 seconds.

- Add the stock, vermouth, lemon, basil, thyme, tomatoes, fennel seeds, salt, pepper, and clams. Cover and cook until most of the clams are open. Do not overcook. Discard unopened clams. Divide the clams among 4 hot bowls and keep warm.

- Add the lemon butter to the broth in the pot and swirl until it melts. Divide the mixture among clam bowls. Garnish with croutons and parsley.

Serves four

Oysters in Saffron Cream with Caviar

Jack Amon, Marx Bros. Cafe

Alaska oysters are grown in stacked nets called lantern nets that hang in the icy water. Because the oysters aren't fighting the tides or predators on the beach, they can put energy into growing meat rather than shell. The result is an oyster with a deep cup full of steely, crisp meat. Pour a flute of Champagne and serve these rich, beautiful oysters for a special occasion. Caviar gives the oysters an extra-elegant touch. If money is tight, they can be served without the caviar, but they are so much nicer with it.

> 24 large oysters
> 1½ cups dry Champagne or sparkling wine
> Pinch of saffron threads
> 1½ cups heavy cream
> 6 tablespoons butter, cut into 1-tablespoon pieces
> Salt and ground white pepper
> 2 ounces sevruga caviar

- Preheat the oven to 250°F.

- Shuck the oysters and leave in the 24 cups. Place the 24 shell bottoms on a pan lined with parchment paper and place in the oven.

- Bring the Champagne to a boil in a small saucepan. Add the saffron and reduce by a third.

- Add the cream and reduce until quite thick. Turn off the heat and add the oysters. Shake in the pan and let stand for 2 to 3 minutes.

- Place the oysters in the heated shells. Return the sauce to the heat. Reduce until thick. Remove from the heat. Whisk in the butter, piece by piece. When all butter is incorporated, taste for seasoning and add salt and pepper to taste.

- Divide the oysters among 6 plates. Spoon the sauce over the oysters. Top each with an equal amount of caviar. Serve right away.

> Serves six

Ricotta Dungeness Crab Cakes

Kirk McLean, Fiddlehead Restaurant and Bakery

The ricotta cheese lightens up the crab cakes and is mild enough to let the flavor of the crab shine through. Make sure you leave enough time to let the crab cakes chill completely before popping them into a hot pan.

1 cup Dungeness or blue crabmeat, rinsed if salted
½ cup ricotta cheese, drained
½ cup panko (Japanese bread crumbs, available in Asian markets and some supermarkets)
1 tablespoon chopped parsley
1½ teaspoons minced shallots
1 teaspoon dry mustard
1 tablespoon olive oil
½ teaspoon ground white pepper
1 egg
Vegetable oil
½ cup buttermilk
¾ cup cornstarch

■ Pick over the crabmeat to remove any pieces of cartilage. Check to see if salt has been added to crabmeat. If it has, rinse thoroughly. Squeeze dry.

■ Combine gently the crabmeat, ricotta, panko, parsley, shallots, mustard, olive oil, pepper, and egg. Form into 4 patties, place on a plate, and refrigerate overnight or at least 2 hours.

■ Pour enough vegetable oil into a skillet so that it will come halfway up the sides of the cakes when fried. Heat to 350°F.

■ Dip each cake into buttermilk, then into cornstarch. Fry each side until golden brown, about 3 minutes on each side. Drain on paper towels. Serve right away.

Serves four

Salmon Croquettes with Jalapeño Aïoli

Farrokh Larijani, Glacier BrewHouse

Most Alaskan cooks will tell you their summer menus always have room for good ways to use leftover salmon. This is a comforting, homey dish that puts all that extra fish to good use.

SALMON MIXTURE
1½ cups fresh salmon, cooked and flaked
2 tablespoons finely diced onion
½ cup (packed) grated pepper Jack cheese
2 tablespoons mayonnaise
2 teaspoons minced jalapeño, seeded if you like
1½ teaspoons minced chipotle chile
1 tablespoon chopped cilantro
½ teaspoon kosher salt
1 tablespoon minced red pepper
1 egg white, lightly beaten
2 tablespoons panko (Japanese bread crumbs, available in Asian markets and some supermarkets)

BREADING
Peanut or vegetable oil
1 cup panko
1 cup cornmeal
4 egg whites, lightly beaten

GARNISH
12 avocado slices
1 cup Marinated Cabbage (page 20)
4 tablespoons Jalapeño Aïoli (page 20)
4 lemon wedges
8 sprigs of cilantro

■ Gently mix together the salmon, onion, cheese, mayonnaise, jalapeño, chipotle, cilantro, salt, and red pepper until well combined. Add the egg white and 2 tablespoons panko and combine. Shape into 4 patties. Refrigerate for at least 1 hour.

- Heat the oil to 350°F in a pan deep enough so the oil comes halfway up the sides of the croquettes.

- Mix the 1 cup panko and cornmeal together. Dip croquettes into the 4 egg whites, then press into panko-cornmeal mixture. Pan-fry croquettes in oil until golden on each side. Drain on paper towels. Keep warm.

- Fan out 3 avocado slices on each plate and top with ¼ cup cabbage. Place 1 tablespoon aïoli at the base of each cabbage mound. Place a croquette on top of each dollop of aïoli. Garnish each plate with a lemon wedge and cilantro sprigs and serve.

Serves four

Marinated Cabbage

¼ cup rice wine vinegar
2 tablespoons sugar
1 cup red cabbage, finely shredded

- Combine the vinegar and sugar and whisk until the sugar is dissolved. Add the cabbage and mix well. Refrigerate.

Makes 1 cup

Jalapeño Aïoli

1 cup mayonnaise
½ teaspoon minced garlic
¼ teaspoon cayenne
1½ tablespoons minced jalapeño
¼ cup minced red onion
1 teaspoon grated lime zest
1 tablespoon chopped cilantro
¼ teaspoon kosher salt
Pinch of black pepper
Juice of ½ lime
½ teaspoon chile powder

- Mix all ingredients together well. Refrigerate.

Makes 1⅓ cups

Savory Custards with Garlic Sauce

Jennifer Jolis, Jennifer's

To Alaskans who live in the bush, Fairbanks is a big city visited to get supplies and fuel. To Alaskans who live in Anchorage, Fairbanks is considered less than a culinary Mecca. But both sorts of Alaskans and a whole generation of Fairbanks residents discovered how good savory custards could be when Jolis served these at her namesake restaurant, Jennifer's.

> 2 teaspoons butter
> 1¼ cups milk
> 1¼ cups heavy cream
> 1 teaspoon minced fresh rosemary
> 2 teaspoons minced fresh thyme
> 2 bay leaves
> 5 cloves garlic, peeled and crushed
> 3 eggs
> Pinch of grated nutmeg
> Pinch of kosher salt
> Pinch of ground white pepper
> Garlic Sauce (page 22)
> 4 sprigs of rosemary

- Preheat oven to 350°F.

- Butter four 4-ounce ramekins with 2 teaspoons butter.

- Combine the milk, cream, rosemary, thyme, bay, and garlic in a medium saucepan. Bring to a simmer, then adjust heat to gently simmer for 45 minutes, or until the liquid reduces by a fourth. Set aside to cool for 15 minutes.

- Whisk the eggs in a large bowl until the whites and yolks are just combined. Strain the milk mixture into a separate bowl, pressing the solids to extract all the flavor. Slowly whisk the milk mixture into the eggs, being careful not to whip too much air into the mixture. Add the nutmeg, salt, and pepper. Divide the mixture equally among the ramekins.

- Place the ramekins in a baking tray at least 1 inch deep. Pour hot water around the ramekins until the water level is halfway up the side of the ramekins. Cover the ramekins with parchment or wax paper and bake until the custard is just set, about 25 minutes.

■ Carefully run a knife around the edge of the custard. Place a small plate upside down over the custard and quickly invert. If the custard does not immediately come out, hold the ramekin on the plate with your thumbs and tap the plate and ramekin once or twice sharply on the counter top. Pour the Garlic Sauce around, top with a sprig of rosemary, and serve.

Serves four

Garlic Sauce

2 tablespoons minced shallots
2 cloves garlic, minced
7 tablespoons butter, cut into pieces
1 teaspoon minced fresh rosemary
¼ teaspoon minced fresh thyme
2 tablespoons minced parsley
¼ teaspoon salt
Pinch of freshly ground black pepper

■ Place the shallots and garlic in small saucepan and add 1 tablespoon of the butter. Cook over medium heat and stir until the shallots and garlic are soft. Turn off the heat and swirl in the remaining 6 tablespoons of butter until it just melts, add the rosemary, thyme, parsley, salt, and pepper and blend.

Makes ⅔ cup

Vodka-Cured Gravlax

Jack Amon, Marx Bros. Cafe

Russian settlers had a great influence on Alaska, and that heritage is reflected in the dishes Alaska's chefs choose to show off outside of the state. This is an appetizer of Scandinavian/Russian origin that Amon served at the James Beard House in New York City. Experiment with different types of fish cured in different toppings. Arctic char goes well with mint, and Copper River red salmon is nice with fennel.

> 3 pounds silver salmon fillet, skinned
> ¼ cup vodka
> 1 tablespoon crushed white peppercorns
> ½ cup roughly chopped dill
> 2 tablespoons kosher salt
> 2 tablespoons sugar
> ¼ cup Honey Mustard Sauce (page 24)
> 4 Potato Pancakes, quartered (page 24)
> ½ cup Sour Cream Dill Sauce (page 24)
> ¼ cup smoked salmon caviar
> Sprigs of dill, for garnish

- To make gravlax, coat the flesh of both sides of the salmon with the vodka and then the pepper. Place the salmon, skin side down, in a pan large enough to hold the fillet without bending. Sprinkle dill over salmon, then salt and sugar. Cover the salmon with aluminum foil and weigh it down with a board and a 5-pound weight. Refrigerate for 48 to 72 hours, turning the salmon and basting every 12 hours with accumulated juices.

- Remove the salmon from the pan and pat dry. Wrap in plastic wrap and refrigerate until ready to serve (up to 2 days).

- Thinly slice the gravlax on the diagonal, 3 to 4 slices per person. Roll the slices into 4 rose shapes. Set aside in refrigerator.

- With a squirt bottle filled with honey mustard sauce, squeeze out a flower pattern with the sauce on each of 4 cold plates. Place a salmon rose on the sauce.

- Arrange the potato pancake wedges around the salmon rose. Drizzle the pancakes with sour cream dill sauce. Sprinkle the caviar on top of the sauce. Garnish with dill sprigs.

    Serves four

Honey Mustard Sauce

⅓ cup honey
1 tablespoon Dijon mustard
2 teaspoons finely chopped dill

■ Combine all the ingredients and place in a squeeze bottle. Refrigerate.

Makes ½ cup

Sour Cream Dill Sauce

1 cup heavy cream
¼ cup sour cream
Juice of 1 lemon
1 tablespoon rice wine vinegar
3 tablespoons chopped dill
Freshly ground black pepper

■ Combine ingredients and chill.

Makes 1½ cups

Potato Pancakes

1 large boiling potato, peeled and coarsely grated
Juice of 1 lemon
2 tablespoons minced shallots
1 tablespoon minced garlic
2 tablespoons minced parsley
1 egg, beaten
2 tablespoons flour
¼ teaspoon salt
Pinch of ground black pepper
2 tablespoons vegetable oil

■ Put the grated potato in a bowl with the lemon juice mixed with 2 cups water. Swirl, drain and squeeze the potatoes dry.

- Mix the potatoes in the bowl with the shallots, garlic, parsley, egg, flour, salt, and pepper. Heat a sauté pan over medium heat with the oil until the oil shimmers.

- For each pancake fry about $1/4$ cup of the mixture formed into a $2^1/_2$-inch circle until it is browned on one side. Flip the pancake over and brown the other side. Drain on paper towels. Cut into wedges.

Makes about six pancakes

Salmon Caviar

Alaska chefs use the glistening orange-red eggs of salmon in many ways. The eggs can be eaten fresh, but many Alaska chefs make their own caviar. The treated eggs are wonderful as a garnish for salmon dishes or served plain on good crackers with a little cream cheese or on the tips of endive leaves that have been painted with a little crème fraîche. The trick is to get the membrane separated from the eggs. Chefs use a variation of a basic method that involves breaking the egg sacs with their hands and separating the eggs into a bowl. Some chefs rub the sacs over a square of wire mesh with holes big enough for the eggs to drop through. The eggs sit for an hour or even or a day or two in a salt-water solution. Lemon, vodka, or soy sauce can be added to the brine. Some cooks use a little sugar or honey. A gentle rinse with fresh water and the caviar is ready to go.

Eggplant Pâté

Sean Maryott, The Homestead

This pâté may be used as a dip, spread, or stuffing. It is an easy appetizer, served with baguette slices or crackers.

> 1 eggplant
> 1 head garlic
> 1 tablespoon olive oil
> 3 tablespoons grated parmesan
> 1 tablespoon fresh lemon juice
> 1 teaspoon sea salt
> 1 teaspoon freshly ground Szechuan peppercorns
> ⅔ cup chèvre

- Preheat the oven to 350°F.

- Pierce the eggplant in several places and roast until totally soft, turning once. Peel.

- Slice the top off the head of garlic so that all of the cloves are exposed. Wrap the garlic with the olive oil in aluminum foil. Roast for 40 minutes. Squeeze the cloves out from the skin and discard skin.

- Place the peeled eggplant, roasted garlic, parmesan, lemon juice, salt, and ground peppercorns in a food processor and process until smooth. Add the chèvre and process until smooth.

  Makes 2¼ cups

Wild Mushroom Tart

Jack Amon, Marx Bros. Cafe

Shaggy manes, morels, boletes, puffballs, and hedgehogs all grow in Southcentral Alaska. This is a very popular appetizer that can easily double as an entrée at lunch. You can substitute a mix of different domestic mushrooms if you can't find wild mushrooms, but wild are best.

2 tablespoons butter
1 large onion, sliced thin
1 tablespoon cider vinegar
3 eggs
¼ cup whole milk
½ cup heavy cream
⅛ teaspoon salt
⅛ teaspoon white pepper
¼ teaspoon nutmeg, grated
One 5-inch prebaked Tart Shell (page 28)
¼ cup (tightly packed) grated Gruyère or Swiss cheese
4 ounces fresh wild mushrooms, sliced thin
1 tablespoon chopped fresh thyme with flowers

- Preheat the oven to 350°F.

- Melt 1 tablespoon of the butter in a heavy skillet over medium-low heat. Add the onion and cook until light brown. Add the vinegar and continue cooking until light caramel color. Set aside.

- In mixing bowl, gently whisk together the eggs, milk, and cream. Add the salt, pepper, and nutmeg and combine.

- Spread the caramelized onions evenly over the bottom of the baked tart shell. Cover with grated cheese, then mushrooms. Pour the egg mixture over the mushrooms, being careful not to fill it over the lip of the shell. Sprinkle the thyme on top. Melt the remaining 1 tablespoon of butter and brush the mushrooms with it from time to time while the tart bakes. Bake 25 to 30 minutes, or until custard is just set.

Serves four

Tart Shell

½ cup flour
¼ teaspoon salt
¼ teaspoon sugar
3 tablespoons butter, chilled
1 egg yolk
1½ teaspoons sour cream

■ Preheat the oven to 375°F.

■ Mix together the flour, salt, and sugar. Add the butter. With a pastry cutter or 2 knives, cut the butter into the flour mixture until it resembles cornmeal. In a separate small bowl, mix together the egg yolk and sour cream. Add to flour mixture. Mix together until it is well blended and holds together. Press into a ball, wrap with plastic wrap, and refrigerate for at least 1 hour.

■ Roll out until ⅛ inch thick, and place in a tart pan with a removable bottom. Prick the dough lightly with a fork. Fill with pastry weights or dried beans and bake for 10 minutes.

■ Remove the weights and return to the oven for 5 minutes more, or until the crust is lightly browned.

Makes one 5-inch shell, ½ inch deep

Zucchini Pancakes with Cambozola

Jennifer Jolis, Jennifer's

This is one of two appetizers Jolis served at the Alaska dinner at the James Beard House in New York City. It represents the end of summer and the beginning of fall in interior Alaska, and a melding of the wild and cultivated bounty it has to offer.

> 7 tablespoons all-purpose flour
> 1 teaspoon sugar
> 3 tablespoons grated parmesan
> ⅓ teaspoon salt
> 1 teaspoon baking powder
> ¼ teaspoon grated nutmeg
> Pinch of ground black pepper
> 1 egg
> ½ cup milk
> 1½ tablespoons butter, melted
> 1 cup grated zucchini
> Vegetable oil spray
> 2 tablespoons wild lowbush cranberries or regular cranberries
> 1 ounce Cambozola cheese, at room temperature

- Gently whisk together the flour, sugar, parmesan, salt, baking powder, nutmeg, and pepper in a large bowl. In a different bowl, whisk together the egg, milk, and butter.

- Place the zucchini on a tea towel, roll it up, and wring it out until all the moisture is squeezed out. Stir the zucchini into the egg mixture. Fold the zucchini mixture into the flour mixture until just combined.

- Heat a nonstick skillet over medium heat and spray with vegetable oil spray.

- Add about 3 tablespoons of the batter per pancake. When bubbles appear, sprinkle each pancake with 1 teaspoon of cranberries and turn.

- Serve 2 pancakes per portion topped with a sliver of Cambozola.

> Serves four

Soups, Salads,
and Sandwiches

Alaskan Seafood Chowder

Elizabeth King, Southside Bistro

In France, bouillabaisse is king. In San Francisco, the Italians perfected cioppino. In Alaska, warming fish chowders get people through the winter. Since there is usually a lot of seafood around Alaska kitchens, this stew takes advantage of it. In this recipe, you can substitute whatever sort of sturdy fish might be available, but Alaska salmon is best.

Chef King is an advocate of seasoning at every step. Don't wait until the very end to add salt and pepper. It will create more depth in flavor if you season as you go. Always add a little salt when sautéing vegetables. It will allow them to release their flavors to the fullest.

2 pounds Alaskan steamer clams, scrubbed

½ teaspoon salt

Pinch of ground black pepper

1 tablespoon chopped garlic

1 tablespoon chopped shallots

2 cups steaming liquid, such as Fish Stock (page 200), white wine, or water

2 ribs celery, finely diced

1 white onion, finely diced

½ carrot, peeled, finely diced

2 cloves garlic, minced

2 shallots, minced

⅓ cup flour

1½ teaspoons chopped fresh thyme

1½ tablespoons chopped basil

1½ tablespoons chopped Italian parsley

¾ cup dry white wine

1 cup Fish Stock (page 200) or water

1½ cups heavy cream

1½ tablespoons fresh lemon juice

½ cup cooked sweet corn (fresh, canned, or frozen)

4 ounces Yukon Gold potatoes, diced small

8 ounces Alaskan salmon, diced small

Kosher salt, black pepper, and cayenne

2 tablespoons snipped fresh chives

- Put the clams, salt, pepper, garlic, shallots, and steaming liquid in a large pot. Cover and steam over high heat until most of the clams have opened. Discard any unopened clams. Remove the clams and set aside the broth. When the clams are cool enough to handle, pick the clam meat out and set aside. Discard the clam shells.

- Melt the butter in a large soup pot over medium heat. Add the celery, onion, carrot, garlic, and shallots. Cook until the onions begin to get tender, about 6 minutes. Add the flour, stir well, and continue to cook over medium heat for about 2 minutes without browning the mixture. Add the wine and whisk in with a heavy whisk. Simmer for 2 minutes. Add the reserved clam broth, the fish stock, cream, and lemon juice. Bring to a simmer.

- Add the corn and potatoes. Simmer until the potatoes are tender, about 10 minutes. Add the salmon and reserved clams. Simmer 2 minutes longer. Adjust the seasoning with salt, pepper, and cayenne to taste. Garnish with chives and serve.

Serves four as an entrée or six to eight as a starter

Southside Black Bean Soup

Jens Nannestad, Southside Bistro

Alaska is a land of travelers and cultures. It isn't unheard of to find people from Latin American countries and the Caribbean who traveled north seeking fortune and adventure. Thus, the flavors of those countries don't seem out of place. This soup is almost always a sellout at the Bistro. Lime juice gives it extra brightness.

2 cups dried black beans
2 tablespoons vegetable oil
½ red onion, diced
½ white onion, diced
1 stalk celery, diced
2 tablespoons chopped garlic
2 tablespoons chopped shallots
3 tablespoons chopped cilantro
2 ripe tomatoes, chopped
2 tablespoon chopped green onion
1 jalapeño, seeded if desired, chopped
1 teaspoon ground dried chipotle chile
½ cup white wine
4 cups Chicken Stock (page 197) or canned chicken broth
Seasonings, such as ground coriander, ground cumin, chile powder,
    black pepper, kosher salt, lemon juice, and lime juice

GARNISH
Salsa
Sour cream
Sprigs of cilantro
Fried tortilla strips

- Soak the beans in water for 24 hours. Drain and rinse.

- Heat the oil in a soup pot over medium-high heat. Sauté the onions and celery until just tender, about 5 minutes. Reduce the heat, add the garlic and shallots, and cook 1 minute. Add the beans, cilantro, tomatoes, green onions, jalapeño, chipotle, wine, and stock and bring to a simmer. Cook until the beans are tender, about 1 hour.

- Remove half of the soup and purée in a food processor. Return the puréed soup to the pot. Add seasonings to taste.

■ Serve hot with garnishes of salsa, sour cream, cilantro sprigs, and fried tortilla strips.

Serves ten

The Ethnic Influence

On paper, Alaska doesn't seem ethnically diverse. Census data show almost two thirds of the population is Caucasian. But the state—and particularly its biggest city, Anchorage—is something of a cultural crossroads, and the influence of different culinary traditions is evident in the dishes served in many of Alaska's restaurants.

You'll find some of the nation's best sushi in Anchorage, partly because the city was a stopover for flights to and from the Far East. The state also enjoys relatively quick access to the fish of Hawaii and Japan. That, coupled with the pristine nature of Alaska's wild fish, make for superb sashimi and sushi. If you visit Anchorage, drop in at Tempura Kitchen (3826 Spenard Road, 907-277-2741) and see for yourself.

And if you're in town, be sure to try some of the city's Korean restaurants. The city has a substantial Korean population, which began when Korea War veterans who had been stationed in Alaska married Korean women. Many moved back to Alaska, and families followed. Anchorage's Korea House (3337 Fairbanks Street, 907-276-5188) is a favorite of Korean Air flight crews and good place to experience the best of the state's Korean restaurants.

Even in small, rural towns the impact of immigrants can be seen. You can eat Vietnamese food in Dutch Harbor, Chinese food in Nome, and if you find yourself in Barrow, make sure to stop in at Pepe's North of the Border Restaurant (1204 Agvik Street, 907-852-8200). In southeast Alaska, you'll find strong Scandinavian influences in towns like Petersburg.

The sturdy food of Russia also has influenced the way Alaskans eat. Little Diomede Island off the west coast of Alaska is only 2.5 miles from Russia's Big Diomede Island and parts of the state were once under the Russian flag. Fish pies, potato dishes, cabbage salads, and preserved mushroom recipes all reflect that heritage.

The food of Alaska's Eskimo and Indian population, who make up about 17 percent of the state, is also reflected in the extensive use of wild berries and preserved fish. The myriad fish treatments on menus throughout the state echo methods of drying and smoking salmon and other fish that have been used by Native Alaskans for thousands of years.

Chilled Fruit Soup

Mark Linden, Glacial Reflections Catering

Alaskans crave fruit in the summer—perhaps because the intense, seasonal flavor of melons and berries helps Alaskans make the most of the short summer season. This is a cool summer soup that makes a nice dish for a brunch or can also be enjoyed as a dessert. And if you're willing to pay the price for imported fruit in the middle of an Alaskan winter, it is a nice reminder of sunnier days.

2 tablespoons sugar
1 tablespoon rice vinegar
1 cup apple cider
1 tablespoon pickling spice
¼ cup crème de menthe
¼ cup chopped mint
1½ cups apple juice
1 cup orange juice
1 cup pineapple juice
½ small honeydew melon, peeled, seeded, and chopped
½ small cantaloupe, peeled, seeded, and chopped
4 small white potatoes, peeled and chopped
½ small honeydew melon, peeled, seeded, and diced, for garnish
½ small cantaloupe, peeled, seeded, and diced, for garnish
4 mint leaves

- Put the sugar and vinegar in large saucepan. Place on medium heat and cook until light golden brown, not stirring, about 8 minutes. Carefully add the cider, pickling spice, crème de menthe, and mint; there will be steam from the hot pan. Bring to a simmer and reduce by a third. Add the apple, orange, and pineapple juices, the chopped honeydew and cantaloupe melons, and potatoes, bring to a simmer, and cook until the potatoes are very tender, about 15 minutes.

- Purée the melon mixture in a blender or food processor and strain. Set aside the liquid, discarding the solids. Refrigerate the liquid until thoroughly chilled.

- Divide the soup among 4 chilled bowls, garnish with diced melon and fresh mint leaves, and serve.

Serves four

Gazpacho with Dungeness Crab

Jennifer Jolis, Jennifer's

In parts of Southwest and Southcentral Alaska, where crab is abundant, Dungeness can turn up in all sorts of surprising places. Even in Fairbanks, a city in Alaska's interior far from the crabbing grounds, Dungeness crab is common. Here, Jolis mixes crab with the light, refreshing flavors of a traditional gazpacho. Depending on your preference, this soup may be puréed or left chunky or be a combination of each. Jolis prefers it entirely puréed.

1 clove garlic, minced
1 medium onion, cut in small dice
1 cucumber, peeled and seeded, cut in small dice
4 cups fire-roasted or high-quality canned tomatoes, with juice
1 green pepper, seeds and veins removed, cut in small dice
¼ serrano chile, seeds removed, minced
¼ teaspoon salt
2 tablespoons balsamic vinegar
2 tablespoons red wine vinegar
¼ cup olive oil
1½ teaspoons (packed) chopped cilantro
8 tablespoons sour cream
8 ounces Dungeness crabmeat, picked over, rinsed if salted
½ cup balsamic vinegar, reduced to 2 to 3 tablespoons

- Purée the garlic, onion, cucumber, tomatoes, green pepper, and serrano in a food processor or heavy-duty blender. With the machine running, add the salt, 2 tablespoons balsamic vinegar, the red wine vinegar, and olive oil. Refrigerate until thoroughly chilled.

- To serve, divide the soup among 8 chilled bowls. Sprinkle with cilantro. Add 1 tablespoon of sour cream per bowl, then top with 1 ounce of crabmeat. Drizzle the reduced balsamic vinegar over all by dipping a fork in it and waving it back and forth over the bowl. Serve right away.

Serves eight

Onion Borscht

Kirsten Dixon, Riversong Lodge

Russian food is a favorite topic of Dixon's. Russian explorers were the first known white men to set foot in Alaska in 1741. They set up the first non-Native towns and trading centers. More than a century later, the United States bought Alaska from Russia for $7.2 million. With all that history, food with Russian influences makes sense on Alaskan tables. Dixon respects the history, but she also has lots of easy-to-store beets and onions on hand—essential elements of Russian cooking. This is her loose interpretation of borscht. It is meant to be a first-course accompaniment to a heavy meal such as beef tenderloin.

> 3 large beets, scrubbed
> 4 tablespoons (½ stick) butter
> Salt and ground black pepper
> 2¾ cups Rich Beef Broth (page 40)
> 2 medium-size sweet onions (such as Vidalia), peeled
> 1 teaspoon freshly grated nutmeg
> 1 tablespoon chopped fresh oregano
> ¼ cup sour cream

- Preheat the oven to 400°F.

- Rub the beets with 2 tablespoons of the butter and sprinkle with salt and pepper. Wrap the beets individually in aluminum foil and place them on a small baking pan large enough to hold them comfortably. Add ¼ cup of the beef broth diluted with a little water to the bottom of the pan. Place the pan in the center of the oven and bake for 1 hour, or until the beets are tender. Set aside to cool.

- Quarter the onions, liberally salt and pepper them, and spread with the remaining 2 tablespoons butter. Place the onions in a small baking dish large enough to hold them comfortably. Sprinkle the onions with nutmeg and oregano. Add enough of the remaining beef broth to cover the bottom of the pan. Cover with aluminum foil and place in the center of the oven and bake until tender, about 20 minutes.

- Remove the skin of the beets by rubbing with paper or cloth towel. Chop 1 beet into small dice and quarter the remaining two.

- Place the remaining 2½ cups beef broth in a medium saucepan over medium heat. Add the diced beet. Reduce the heat and simmer for 10 minutes. Strain the broth, discarding diced beet.

- To serve, place 2 onion quarters and 2 beet quarters into each of 4 warmed wide-rimmed shallow bowls. Divide the hot broth among the bowls. Serve the sour cream on the side.

Serves four

Rich Beef Broth

¼ cup vegetable oil
2 pounds beef bones, cut into ½-inch lengths
¾ cup chopped onion
½ cup chopped carrot
½ cup chopped celery
2 quarts Beef Stock (page 198)
1 small leek, white and light green part, thinly sliced

- Preheat oven to 400°F.

- Pour oil into a small roasting pan and place in oven for 10 minutes. Add bones, toss, and roast until browned all over, about 20 minutes. Add onion, carrot, and celery. Roast for another 10 minutes.

- Remove bones and vegetables from the roasting pan and place in a saucepan. Discard remaining oil in the pan. Add 1 cup of stock to the pan. With a wooden spoon, scrape up any brown bits in the pan and add the stock–brown bit mixture and the leek to the saucepan.

- Over medium-high heat, bring the broth to a simmer. Adjust heat to maintain a simmer and cook for 4 hours. Strain broth; discard solids.

- If not using broth immediately, cool in an ice bath. Refrigerate for up to 2 days or freeze for a later use.

Makes 1 quart

Oscar's Chowder

Mark Linden, Glacial Reflections Catering

Some of Alaska's traditionally trained chefs stay true to classics, but with a twist. This recipe was inspired by the classical Oscar garnish made from fresh tarragon, crab, and asparagus.

1 pound asparagus
4 tablespoons (½ stick) butter
2 tablespoons olive oil
½ cup sliced carrots
¼ cup sliced celery
½ cup sliced onion
1 Granny Smith apple, peeled, cored, and sliced
1 pear, peeled, cored, and sliced
½ teaspoon salt
¼ teaspoon ground white pepper
2 tablespoons dried tarragon
¾ pound red potatoes, peeled and sliced
¼ cup plus 3 tablespoons dry sherry
2½ cups Chicken Stock (page 197) or high-quality unsalted broth
¾ cup heavy cream
8 ounces Dungeness crabmeat, picked over, rinsed if salted
2 tablespoons chopped fresh tarragon

■ Cut the tips off the asparagus and set the tips and stems aside separately.

■ Heat the butter and oil into a large saucepan over medium heat until the butter melts. Add the reserved asparagus stems, the carrots, celery, onion, apple, pear, salt, pepper, and dried tarragon and stir. Cover and cook over medium-low heat for 10 to 15 minutes, or until the vegetables are soft.

■ Add the potatoes, the ¼ cup of sherry, and the stock, bring to a simmer, and cook until the potatoes are very soft. Place the mixture in a food processor or mixer and purée. Strain, reserving the liquid.

■ In another saucepan, reduce the remaining 3 tablespoons sherry by half. Add the cream and crabmeat, bring to a simmer, and reduce slightly.

- Steam the reserved asparagus tips until just tender.

- Add the reserved liquid to the crab mixture, bring to a boil, and add the fresh tarragon. Season to taste with additional salt and white pepper. Garnish with asparagus tips and serve.

Serves four

Potato–Green Chile Soup

JoAnn Asher, Sacks Cafe

Like cooking in much of the rest of the country, Alaska's cuisine went through a Southwest phase. This soup originally came out of the period in the late 1980s and early 1990s when the chiles, cumin, and other flavors from Arizona and New Mexico were common. It remains a favorite at Sacks Cafe, even though it doesn't turn up on the menu as much as it used to. Still, people always ask for the recipe when it does.

4 medium potatoes, peeled and cubed
3½ cups Chicken Stock (page 197) or Vegetable Stock (page 199)
1 tablespoon butter
1 tablespoon olive oil
1 cup diced onion
½ cup diced red pepper
1 teaspoon minced garlic
1 teaspoon salt
½ teaspoon ground cumin
1 teaspoon dried oregano
1 teaspoon ground coriander
¾ cup half-and-half
⅓ cup diced canned green chiles
¼ cup grated sharp cheddar
¼ cup grated Monterey Jack

■ Cover the potatoes with stock in a large saucepan, bring to a simmer, and cook until the potatoes are tender. Process in a food processor until the potatoes are puréed. Return the potato-stock mixture to the saucepan and keep warm.

■ Heat the butter and oil in a skillet over medium heat until they sizzle. Add the onion, red pepper, and garlic and cook until the onion and pepper are soft. Add the salt, cumin, oregano, and coriander. Add the onion mixture to the potato mixture and mix well. Add the half-and-half and chiles. Taste and adjust the seasonings.

■ Heat the soup until it steams, then divide among 4 hot soup bowls. Garnish with cheeses and serve.

Serves four

Smoked Halibut Chowder

Jennifer Jolis, Jennifer's

If you're lucky enough to go halibut fishing, chances are you will come home with 30 pounds of meat or more—sometimes much more. The firm white meat takes well to the flavor of smoke, and so many Alaskans preserve some of their catch by having it professionally smoked or using a small home smoker. This hearty chowder offers a unique way to use the result. Other sturdy smoked fish may be used.

3 tablespoons butter
2½ tablespoons flour
¼ cup diced green bell pepper
¼ cup diced red bell pepper
½ cup diced leeks, white parts only
¼ cup finely diced onion
⅓ cup diced carrot
1 stalk celery, diced
1 cup peeled and diced boiling potato
2 cups Fish Stock (page 200) or clam juice
¾ cup water
½ bay leaf
1 cup heavy cream
6 ounces smoked halibut, skin and bones removed,
    broken into bite-size pieces
Pinch of ground white pepper
Pinch of cayenne, or less
Salt
4 lemon slices
2 tablespoons chopped parsley

■ Melt 2 tablespoons of the butter in a small saucepan over low heat. Stir in the flour with a whisk. With a wooden spoon, continue to stir for 3 minutes. Do not brown the roux. Set aside.

■ Simmer red and green peppers for 5 minutes in a small pot of boiling water. Drain and set aside.

- Melt 1 tablespoon of butter in a soup pot and gently cook the leeks, onion, carrots, and celery until soft. Add the potatoes, stock, water, and $\frac{1}{2}$ bay leaf and bring to a boil. Reduce to a simmer and cook until the potatoes are tender.

- Whip the roux into the soup, then bring the soup back to a simmer. Cook for 3 minutes. Reduce the heat to low. Add the cream, halibut, white pepper, cayenne, and reserved red and green bell peppers. Taste and adjust seasoning with salt.

- Divide the chowder among 4 large, hot soup bowls. Garnish each with a lemon slice and parsley.

Serves four

Cream of Alaskan Summer Squash and Fresh Sweet Basil Soup

Jens Nannestad, Southside Bistro

Summer is short, but the days are long. Thus, gardeners experience amazing results with squash, lettuce, and peas. And as for gardeners everywhere, too much zucchini can be a problem. This soup makes the best of the situation. The fresh basil really highlights the vegetables.

2 tablespoons olive oil
2 large zucchini, diced
2 large yellow squash, diced
½ red onion, diced
½ white onion, diced
2 ribs celery, diced
2 tablespoons chopped garlic
1 cup white wine
3 cups Chicken Stock (page 197) or canned chicken broth
2 cups heavy cream
½ cup chopped basil
Seasonings, such as kosher salt, ground black pepper,
    crushed red pepper, cayenne
¼ cup pistachio nuts, toasted and roughly chopped

- Heat the olive oil in a soup pot over medium heat. Add the zucchini, yellow squash, onions, celery, and garlic and stir. Cover and cook for 5 to 10 minutes without browning any of the vegetables. Add the wine, stock, and cream and simmer for 30 minutes.

- Purée the soup in a food processor, return to the pot, and heat over medium heat until hot. Whisk in the basil and add seasonings to your liking.

- Divide among 4 large, warm soup bowls. Garnish with pistachios and serve.

Serves four

Tomato Bisque

Jennifer Jolis, Jennifer's

This soup takes us back to childhood while still satisfying our adult tastes. It's also easy to make it completely vegetarian—just substitute olive or vegetable oil for the bacon. The taste will be slightly different, but still good.

It is very important to heat the cream and add it to the tomatoes slowly. This prevents it from curdling when it comes in contact with the acid of the tomatoes.

> 2 ounces bacon, diced
> 2 cloves garlic, minced
> ¾ cup finely chopped onion
> 12 ounces canned diced tomatoes in juice
> 6 tablespoons tomato paste
> ½ bay leaf
> ½ teaspoon dried thyme
> 2 cups heavy cream
> Seasoning, such as salt, ground pepper, and sugar
> 1 tablespoon chopped fresh basil

- Cook the bacon pieces in a small, heavy-duty soup pot over medium-high heat until they render their fat and are crisp. Remove from the heat. Remove the bacon pieces and reserve for another use.

- Return the pot to low heat and cook the garlic and onion until soft. Add the tomatoes and their juices and the tomato paste and stir to combine. Add the ½ bay leaf and thyme and bring to a simmer. Reduce the heat and simmer for about 30 minutes, being careful not to evaporate all of the moisture.

- In a small saucepan, slowly bring the cream to a scald. Add the cream to the soup base slowly, mix in, and taste for seasoning.

- Divide the bisque among 4 hot soup bowls and sprinkle the basil equally over each.

> Serves four

Van's Famous Caesar Salad

Van Hale, Marx Bros. Cafe

This salad was first prepared at Caesar Cardini's restaurant in Tijuana in the late 1920s. Its popularity grew and today the Caesar Salad is an American institution. The version made tableside by the Marx Bros. Cafe's wine steward, Van Hale, is simple. Some versions call for mustard and Worcestershire sauce to jazz it up. Van just uses the finest vinegar, olive oil, anchovies, and imported parmesan cheese.

To make the salad, a good wooden bowl is essential. Season the bowl well with olive oil and never wash it with soap.

> 2 teaspoons plus ¼ cup extra virgin olive oil
> 6 garlic cloves
> 6 anchovy fillets
> 2 eggs, at room temperature
> 1 lemon
> 1 teaspoon aged balsamic vinegar
> 2 tablespoons freshly grated Parmigiano-Reggiano
> 2 large heads of romaine lettuce, washed, torn, and spun dry
> 1 cup croutons
> Freshly ground black pepper

■ Bring a small pan of water to a boil. Add the eggs and boil 1 minute to coddle them. Remove the eggs from the water and set aside.

■ Drizzle the 2 teaspoons olive oil in the bottom of a large wooden bowl. Add the garlic and mash it well with a fork. Add the anchovies and continue to mash until the mixture resembles a fine paste. Using a wooden spoon, mash the garlic-anchovy mixture into the sides and bottom of the bowl.

■ Break the coddled eggs into the bowl, add the juice of the lemon, and mix thoroughly. Add the ¼ cup olive oil and the vinegar and blend.

■ Add the Parmigiano. Add the lettuce and toss the leaves so that they are coated with dressing. Add the croutons and mix well.

■ Serve on a chilled plate and garnish with a sprinkle of Parmigiano and a grind of cracked pepper.

> Serves four

Chinese Chicken Salad

Jennifer Jolis, Jennifer's

This recipe came to Jennifer from a friend, Thede Tobish. It is pretty, tasty, and healthy. What more can you ask of a salad?

8 ounces dried short pasta, such as spirals, elbows, shells, or bow ties
¾ cup broccoli florets, blanched and chilled
¾ cup cooked chicken strips
½ medium red bell pepper, cut into thin strips
2 green onions, cut into ½-inch diagonal lengths
¾ cup snow peas, blanched, chilled, and cut in half

DRESSING
1½ teaspoons peeled and chopped fresh ginger
3 cloves garlic, chopped
2½ tablespoons red wine vinegar
1 tablespoon honey
½ teaspoon Tabasco
6 tablespoons vegetable oil
2 teaspoons sesame oil
Dash of Chinese hot pepper oil
Salt and ground black pepper to taste
1 tablespoon toasted sesame seeds

■ Cook the pasta in 2 quarts of salted boiling water until just done. Rinse under cold running water until cool. Drain thoroughly. Set aside.

■ Cut the broccoli into bite-size pieces. Add the broccoli, chicken, red pepper, green onions, and snow peas to the pasta. Toss to mix.

■ To make the dressing, put the ginger, garlic, vinegar, honey, and Tabasco in a blender and blend at medium speed until the ginger and garlic are smooth. Combine the vegetable oil, sesame oil, and hot pepper oil in a cup. With the blender running, add the oil mixture to the ginger mixture in a thin steady stream. Season with salt and pepper to taste.

■ Add all but ¼ cup of the dressing to the pasta mixture and stir well. Taste and adjust the seasoning. If the salad is not served right away, check right before serving to see if it needs the remaining dressing.

Serves four

Cobb Salad Sandwich

Farrokh Larijani, Glacier BrewHouse

Leave it to an Alaskan to take a relaxed approach to the traditional. The classic American salad, invented in the late 1920s by Bob Cobb, manager of the original Brown Derby in Hollywood, California, is a fixture on many menus. Larijani took the classic and gave it an Alaskan twist. The radish salad provides a crisp and refreshing finish.

DIJON MAYONNAISE
1 cup bottled mayonnaise
¼ cup Dijon mustard
2 ounces Danish blue cheese, crumbled
¾ teaspoon freshly ground black pepper

SANDWICH
8 slices sourdough bread
8 ounces sliced honey baked ham
8 ounces sliced smoked turkey
8 pepper bacon slices, cooked crisp
2 cups iceberg lettuce, shredded
1¼ cups Radish Salad (page 51)
½ ripe avocado, sliced ⅛ inch thick
4 Roma tomatoes, cored and sliced

- To prepare the dijon mayonnaise, combine all the ingredients. Refrigerate.

- To make the sandwiches, toast the bread slices lightly and spread with of the mayonnaise.

- Fold each of the ham and turkey slices and layer them on the bread. Lay the bacon on top of the sliced meat. Top with lettuce, radish salad, avocado slices, and tomatoes and serve.

Serves four

Radish Salad

10 small radishes of any sort, scrubbed and sliced ⅛ inch thick

½ cup sliced (⅛ inch) red onions

1 cup sliced (⅛ inch) English cucumber

¼ cup rice wine vinegar

2 teaspoons sugar

■ Combine all ingredients and mix well. Refrigerate before serving.

Serves four to six

Escalope of Alaskan Salmon With Chive and Lime Salad

Al Levinsohn, Alyeska Resort

Salmon is so common that Alaska chefs have a field day creating new ways to use it. Here, an interesting mix of deep-fried potato croutons and lots of crunchy daikon radish and bell pepper give this hot salad a lively texture.

CITRUS VINAIGRETTE
2 tablespoons orange juice concentrate
2 tablespoons fresh lime juice
2 tablespoons honey
1 tablespoons rice vinegar
1 cup olive oil
Salt and ground black pepper

POTATO CROUTONS
1 baking potato, peeled
Vegetable oil, for frying
Salt and ground black pepper

CHIVE AND LIME SALAD
½ medium red bell pepper, sliced thin
½ medium yellow bell pepper, sliced thin
½ cup thinly sliced red onion
2 limes, peeled and sliced thin
½ cup bean sprouts
½ cup daikon sprouts
½ cup thinly sliced daikon root
½ cup chopped cilantro
2 tablespoons minced fresh chives
2 cups mesclun or spring greens mix

SALMON
4 salmon fillets, 5 ounces each
Salt and ground white pepper
1 tablespoon olive oil

- To prepare the vinaigrette, place the orange juice concentrate, lime juice, honey, and rice vinegar in a blender. With the blender running slowly, add the oil in a thin, steady stream.

- Season with salt and pepper to taste. Refrigerate.

- To prepare the potato croutons, dice enough potato to make $1/2$ cup. Deep-fry in vegetable oil until crisp and golden. Drain, season with salt and pepper, and keep warm.

- Toss together the red and yellow peppers, onion, limes, bean sprouts, daikon sprouts, daikon root, cilantro, and chives in a medium bowl.

- Wash the mesclun mix, drain, and dry.

- Season the salmon fillets with salt and pepper. Heat the olive oil in a skillet over medium-high heat until it shimmers. Pan-fry the salmon until it is just cooked through, a few minutes per side, depending on thickness.

- Add 2 tablespoons of the vinaigrette to the lettuce and toss to coat. Divide the salad among 4 plates. Place a salmon fillet on top of each plate of lettuce.

- Add $1/4$ cup of vinaigrette to the bowl of vegetables and toss to coat. Divide vegetables and place an equal amount on top of each salmon fillet. Season with salt and pepper.

- Drizzle the remaining 2 tablespoons of vinaigrette around the edges of the salad. Top with croutons and serve.

Serves four

Muffaletas

Jennifer Jolis, Jennifer's

These are the most forgiving sandwiches—and they are delicious, too. Forgiving because although they taste better if they are marinated, they are still good if you serve them right away. In addition, you can make them two days ahead of when you need them. They do terrifically at room temperature, cold, or heated. And they are great to take on a hike. At Jennifer's restaurant, they kept a list of people to call on the days they served muffaletas. You'll develop a waiting list, too.

14 ounces pimiento-stuffed green olives, drained and rinsed
8 ounces black olives, pitted, drained, and rinsed
3 cloves garlic
2 tablespoons capers
1 tablespoon dried oregano
1 tablespoon dried basil
$\frac{2}{3}$ teaspoon crushed red pepper
3 tablespoons diced red onion
$\frac{1}{4}$ teaspoon dried savory
1 tablespoon red wine vinegar
3 tablespoons olive oil
4 hoagy rolls
Olive oil for the rolls
1$\frac{1}{2}$ pounds assorted cold cuts, such as Genoa salami, prosciutto, ham, provolone, smoked mozzarella, all thinly sliced

- Chop the green and black olives and the garlic in a food processor. Do not purée. Transfer to a large bowl and add the capers, oregano, basil, red pepper, red onion, savory, vinegar, and olive oil. Mix well.

- Split the hoagy rolls in half. Pull the spongy part of the bread from each side (save the spongy part for bread crumbs), leaving a ½-inch shell of bread on each side. Brush with olive oil.

- Fill each side of the hoagy rolls with 3 to 4 tablespoons of the muffaleta mix.

- Layer the cold cuts and cheese over the olive mixture. Fold the sandwiches back together and wrap each in aluminum foil. If you have time, refrigerate the sandwiches for at least 4 hours and up to 48 hours.

- The sandwich may be served cold or heated in a 375°F oven for 15 to 20 minutes until heated through. Cut each sandwich in half and pierce with toothpicks topped with olives.

Serves four

Purple Potato Salad

Mark Linden, Glacial Reflections Catering

In the Matanuska Valley, a short drive from Anchorage, small farmers are experimenting with potatoes—a crop that does remarkably well in Alaska. Purple potatoes are one of the many successful varieties. This is a colorful and interesting version of potato salad that is simple to make, even in large quantities.

1½ pounds purple potatoes
¼ cup white wine vinegar
¾ cup olive oil
1 tablespoon Dijon mustard
1 small red pepper, seeded and diced small
½ small yellow pepper, seeded and diced small
1 small red onion, diced small
⅓ cup minced cilantro
1 teaspoon salt
¼ teaspoon ground black pepper

■ Wash the potatoes and cook in salted water until tender. Remove and cool slightly. Peel and dice. Place in a large bowl.

■ In a small bowl whisk together the vinegar, oil, and mustard. Fold into the potatoes. Fold in the peppers, onion, cilantro, salt, and pepper. Taste and add more mustard, salt, or pepper if desired. Chill.

Serves six

Grilled Summer Vegetable Salad with Goat Cheese and Pine Nuts

Elizabeth King, Southside Bistro

King, the young chef de cuisine at Southside Bistro, created this Mediterranean-style salad to take advantage of late summer's zucchini and squash harvest. Use any good-quality goat cheese. It really stands up to the grilled vegetables.

2 cloves garlic, minced
2 tablespoons thinly sliced basil
1 tablespoon chopped Italian parsley
2 teaspoons minced fresh oregano
¼ cup balsamic vinegar
¼ cup extra virgin olive oil
Kosher salt and ground black pepper
1 medium zucchini, cut lengthwise into ¼-inch slices
1 medium yellow squash, cut lengthwise into ¼-inch slices
1 medium red onion, cut into ¼-inch slices
1 pound fresh asparagus, tough ends removed
½ pound mushrooms, halved
Kosher salt and ground black pepper
1 roasted red pepper (see page 58), peeled, seeded,
    and cut into thin strips
Olive oil
¼ cup pine nuts, toasted
5 ounces goat cheese

- Preheat the grill.

- Make a vinaigrette in a large bowl by whisking together the garlic, basil, parsley, oregano, vinegar, and extra virgin olive oil. Season with salt and pepper.

- Prepare the zucchini, yellow squash, onion, asparagus, and mushrooms by rubbing them with a little olive oil and seasoning with salt and pepper. Place the vegetables on the grill and mark them before turning. Cook the vegetables until they just begin to get tender, not mushy. The red onions and asparagus will tend to cook more quickly than the others. As the grilled vegetables are done, place them in the vinaigrette with the roasted red peppers and toss to coat.

■ When all of the vegetables are finished cooking, divide the mixture among 4 large bowls. Sprinkle the pine nuts and goat cheese on top.

Serves four

Roasted Peppers

To roast peppers, rub the peppers lightly with olive oil and roast in 400°F oven or on a grill over high heat. Cook until the skin is blistered lightly but do not char completely (this will make them bitter). Turn the peppers to cook on all sides evenly. When blistered on all sides, put the peppers in a bowl and cover tightly with plastic wrap or place in a plastic bag and seal. This will trap in moisture and allow the skin of the pepper to gently steam. Cool the pepper at room temperature for at least 15 minutes. Peel off the skin with a paring knife and remove all seeds and white ribs from inside.

Wildberry Salmon Salad

Kirsten Dixon, Winterlake Lodge

This is an elegant little summer salad that Dixon serves at Winterlake Lodge. She dresses salads with grapeseed oil and a little bit of walnut oil. She also prefers the proper salt and pepper for salads, using fleur de sel or Brittany sea salt and a house pepper mix of black peppercorns, white peppercorns, and allspice.

For the salmon, trim the sides of a fillet so there is a center cut of even thickness about three or four inches across. Red, or sockeye salmon, is Dixon's favorite for salads. Sometimes she marinates cherry tomatoes in balsamic or fig balsamic vinegar, sprinkles them with sea salt, and tosses them into the salad at the last minute.

> 4 center-cut Alaska red salmon fillets, 4 ounces each
> Salt and ground pepper
> ½ cup grapeseed oil
> 6 cups mixed baby green lettuces
> ¼ cup walnut oil
> ¼ cup dried cherries
> ¼ cup fresh berries, such as blueberries or raspberries
> ½ small red onion, diced
> 2 ounces Danish blue cheese, cut into 4 slices

- Chill 4 salad plates.

- Season the salmon fillets with salt and pepper. Heat a medium sauté pan over medium-high heat. Add 1 tablespoon grapeseed oil to the pan and heat until it shimmers. Place 2 fillets, presentation side down, in the pan without crowding and sear for about 2½ minutes. Turn the fillets over and sear the other side for about 2½ minutes more. Remove and keep warm. Repeat with the other 2 fillets.

- Put the greens in a large bowl and toss with just enough grapeseed oil to coat the greens lightly. Drizzle with the walnut oil and toss. The amounts of oil necessary depend on the types of greens used. Lightly season the greens with salt and pepper.

- Place 1½ cups of the dressed greens on the center of each plate. Place a piece of warm salmon on top. Sprinkle the cherries, fresh berries, and red onion around the salad. Top with the blue cheese and serve.

> Serves four

Entrées

Oriental Five-Spice Scallops with Carrot-Ginger-Coconut Sauce

Eric Witt, Sacks Cafe

Diver scallops, or big hand-harvested sea scallops, are all the rage on trendy menus in big cities. In Alaska, sweet, fat Kodiak scallops are nothing new. They are shown off in this dish, which is a hit every time it appears on the menu at Sacks Cafe. The carrot and coconut sauce is a rich and interesting topping for the scallops. Garnish with thin strips of carrot and fresh basil.

> 1 tablespoon butter
> 1 cup sliced carrots
> 1½ teaspoons peeled and chopped fresh ginger
> ½ stalk lemongrass, thinly sliced
> ½ cup Vegetable Stock (page 199) or water
> ½ cup coconut milk
> Salt and ground white pepper
> 24 Kodiak or other sea scallops
> 2 tablespoons five-spice powder
> 2 tablespoons vegetable oil
> 2 tablespoons thin basil strips
> 2 tablespoons julienned carrots

- Melt the butter in a saucepan over medium heat and add the carrots, ginger, and lemongrass. Cook for 4 minutes. Add the stock and heat to a simmer. Cover and finish cooking until the carrots are tender. Purée the carrot mixture in a blender or food processor until smooth.

- Add the coconut milk, blend, and adjust the seasoning with salt and pepper. Return to the saucepan. Keep warm.

- Dust the scallops with the five-spice powder. Heat the oil in a large skillet over medium-high heat until it shimmers. Cook the scallops for 2 minutes on each side. Add more oil if necessary.

- Heat the sauce to a bare simmer and divide among 4 warm plates. Place 6 scallops on each plate, garnish with basil and carrot, and serve.

> Serves four

Alaskan Seafood Gumbo

Al Levinsohn, Alyeska Resort

If you can't get Alaska seafood, this dish allows you to use whatever fish or shellfish might look good at the market. The most difficult part of making a proper gumbo is the cooking of the roux (the mixture of oil and flour that is the thickening agent), which needs to be cooked to the color of an old penny. The trick is not to burn it. If you see black specks in the roux, you will have to repeat the step. Use patience and a long-handled wooden spoon to stir it while cooking so that you don't splatter hot roux on your hands.

½ teaspoon ground white pepper
½ teaspoon cayenne
½ teaspoon ground black pepper
½ teaspoon dried thyme
½ teaspoon dried oregano
4 bay leaves
1 teaspoon kosher salt
¾ cup vegetable oil
¾ cup flour
1 cup diced onion
½ cup diced celery
½ cup diced green bell pepper
1 pound andouille sausage or kielbasa
5 cups Fish Stock (page 200)
1 pound assorted seafood, such as shrimp, crab, salmon, halibut, clams, and mussels
4 cups cooked long-grain rice
4 green onions, thinly sliced

■ Combine the white pepper, cayenne, black pepper, thyme, oregano, bay leaves, and salt and set aside.

■ Heat the oil in a large heavy-duty pot (preferably cast iron) over medium-high heat until it shimmers. Whisk in the flour until smooth. Stir the roux constantly until you obtain the proper brown color. As the roux darkens, reduce the heat to to medium to help protect it from burning.

■ Add the onion, celery, green pepper, and andouille and cook over medium heat until the vegetables are soft. Add 1½ teaspoons of the reserved seasoning, stir, and remove the pan from the heat.

- Add stock carefully (it will sizzle as it touches the hot roux mixture). Let sit for 2 minutes, then incorporate by whisking it in. Return the pot to the stove and bring to a simmer. Cook gently for 30 minutes. Adjust the flavor with the seasoning and more salt if desired. Just prior to service, stir in seafood and cook until just done.

- Divide the rice equally among 4 warm bowls and ladle the gumbo over.

- Garnish with green onions.

Serves four as an entrée or eight as an appetizer

Alder Plank–Roasted Salmon

Jens Hansen, Jens' Restaurant and Bodega

Native Americans have used this cooking method for thousands of years. Hansen used to prepare both fish and meat this way when he first started cooking in Alaska in the 1960s, but stopped for other more "in" ways. It is making a comeback. He does not recommend using the same plank for meat and fish, as flavors set in. To clean the plank, hand-wash and rub it lightly with mineral oil. It should last for your lifetime.

1½ pounds salmon fillet, skin on
1 pound premium butter, such as Plugra
½ cup chopped fresh dill
2 tablespoons fresh lemon juice
½ cup chopped dried berries
1 tablespoon crushed pepper mélange (mixture of black, white, green, and pink peppercorns)
3 tablespoons vegetable oil
1 alder plank

■ Preheat the oven to 400°F.

■ Trim and scale the salmon. Remove the pin bones with tweezers or needle-nosed pliers. Cut the salmon into 4 fillets. Make ⅛-inch cuts through the skin (not into red meat) about 1 inch apart.

■ Place the butter, dill, lemon juice, berries, and pepper mélange in a mixing bowl and beat until light and fluffy. Set aside.

■ Add the oil to a sauté pan large enough to hold the fillets and heat over medium-high heat until the oil shimmers. Sear the fillets, skin side down, for 30 seconds, then remove. Place the fillets, skin side up, on the alder plank. Smear equal portions of the butter mixture evenly over the salmon fillets. Roast the salmon for 8 minutes or until cooked to your likeness.

■ Present the salmon on the plank straight from the oven.

Serves four

Ancho-Encrusted Alaskan Scallops with Angel Hair Pasta in Cilantro Pesto

Mike Holman, Sacks Cafe

Big, meaty sea scallops from Kodiak are best. In any case, ask your fishmonger for what are called hand-harvested or diver scallops.

CILANTRO PESTO
½ cup toasted slivered almonds
⅓ cup canola oil
¼ cup extra virgin olive oil
½ cup chopped cilantro
2 green onions, chopped
1 to 2 jalapeños, seeded and chopped
2 cloves garlic, minced
2 tablespoons fresh lime juice
½ teaspoon salt

SCALLOPS
16 Alaska sea scallops
1 tablespoon ancho chile powder
½ teaspoon sea salt
1 teaspoon dried oregano
1 teaspoon ground cumin
1 teaspoon ground coriander
2 tablespoons vegetable oil

PRESENTATION
½ red bell pepper, cut into ⅛-inch dice
½ yellow or orange bell pepper, cut into ⅛-inch dice
2 jalapeños, seeded and cut into ⅛-inch dice
1 teaspoon minced garlic
Pinch of salt
¼ pound angel hair pasta

- To make the pesto, purée all the ingredients in a food processor or blender. Check for salt to taste.

- To prepare the scallops, rinse the scallops and remove any attaching membrane. Combine the ancho powder, salt, oregano, cumin, and coriander.

- Press both sides of each scallop into the mixture. Pour the oil in a skillet and heat over medium heat until it shimmers. Sear each side of the scallops, removing just before they are cooked completely through, 1 minute or so on each side.

- To make the garnish, combine all the ingredients and set aside.

- Cook the pasta in salted water until al dente. Drain.

- Combine the pesto with the pasta and divide among 4 plates. Arrange 4 cooked scallops on top of each plate of pasta. Sprinkle the garnish on top and serve.

Serves four

Angel Hair Pasta with Crab and Caviar

Jack Amon, Marx Bros. Cafe

This recipe allows you to stretch the crabmeat. If you can't get King crabmeat, other crab can be substituted, but it won't hold its shape as well as King crab.

> 12 ounces angel hair pasta
> 4 ounces (1 stick) butter
> 3 tablespoons finely diced red pepper
> 3 tablespoons finely diced yellow pepper
> 12 ounces King crabmeat, roughly chopped
> Zest of 2 small lemons
> Pinch of salt
> ¼ teaspoon freshly cracked black pepper
> 3 tablespoons minced chives
> 1½ ounces sevruga caviar

- Simmer the pasta until al dente and drain. Shock in cold water, drain, and set aside.

- Melt the butter in a skillet. Add the peppers and crab and lightly sauté. Add the pasta, lemon zest, salt and pepper and stir until pasta heated through. Stir in the chives.

- Divide among 4 heated plates, top with caviar, and serve.

Serves four

Balsamic-Glazed Kodiak Scallops with Tomato Salsa

Elizabeth King, Southside Bistro

The crew at the Southside Bistro has a way with scallops. The trick is searing them in a hot pan or over a hot grill and cooking them only long enough to turn the outside opaque. The inside will continue to cook for a few moments, making the inner flesh just a step past rare—the perfect stage for a scallop. Saffron Risotto Cakes (page 169) are a wonderful accompaniment to this dish.

TOMATO SALSA
8 ounces vine-ripened tomatoes, finely diced

3 tablespoons basil, cut into very thin strips

2 tablespoons parsley, chopped

1 clove garlic, minced

1 tablespoon extra virgin olive oil

2 tablespoons balsamic vinegar

Salt and ground black pepper

SCALLOPS
2 tablespoons finely diced red onion

Salt and ground black pepper

1 ½ cups balsamic vinegar

⅓ cup sugar

1 ½ pounds Kodiak scallops or other sea scallops

Wooden skewers, soaked in water

Olive oil

■ For the salsa, combine the tomatoes, basil, parsley, garlic, extra virgin olive oil, and 2 tablespoons balsamic vinegar in a large bowl. Season with salt and pepper to taste. Set the salsa aside.

■ Simmer the 1½ cups balsamic vinegar and the sugar in a small saucepan until reduced by a third. Cool at room temperature.

■ Preheat the grill until very hot. Skewer the scallops so that they are easier to handle on the grill. Brush the scallops with olive oil and season with 2 teaspoons salt and $1/4$ teaspoon pepper. Grill the scallops for 1 to 2 minutes on each side, or sauté the scallops in olive oil.

■ Arrange the scallops on warm plates and drizzle with balsamic glaze. Garnish with tomato salsa.

Serves four

Barbecued Salmon

David and JoAnn Lesh, Gustavus Inn

In the homey fishing lodge that the Lesh family runs on the edge of Glacier Bay National Park in Southeast Alaska, food has to be on the table quickly when the hungry anglers come back from a day on the water. Luckily, there is usually plenty of fresh fish around to make this simple recipe something special. Halibut fillet can be substituted for salmon with equal success. Leftovers are great in sandwiches, or blended with sour cream, mayonnaise, and dill as a dip for crackers. The Lesh family likes to add some soaked alder chips to the hot coals in order to get a more intensely smoked flavor.

1½ pounds salmon fillet or steak
⅔ cup (packed) brown sugar
Juice of 1 lemon
¼ cup soy sauce
2 sticks butter or margarine
4 lemon wedges

- Cut the salmon into 4 equal fillets or steaks. Leave the skin on.

- Place the brown sugar, lemon juice, soy sauce, and butter in a medium saucepan. Heat the sauce until dissolved and blended.

- Preheat the grill. Grill the salmon fillet, skin side down, over hot coals; do not turn. If steaks are used, they must be turned halfway during the cooking process. Baste the salmon with the sauce 2 to 3 times while cooking; grill the salmon until just done (the flesh should flake easily and should have lost its transparency).

- Serve on heated plates with a lemon wedge and pass the remaining barbecue basting sauce.

Serves four

Halibut Cheeks Braised in Shrimp-Sherry Broth with Leeks, Mushrooms, and Sunchokes

Kirk McLean, Fiddlehead Restaurant and Bakery

Halibut cheeks are common in Alaska and often are given to people working the line at fish processing plants. Your fish market can usually find some, or you can substitute chunks of halibut.

SHRIMP-SHERRY BROTH
1 tablespoon butter
1 medium white onion, diced
2 stalks celery, diced
3 cloves garlic, chopped
8 ounces shrimp shells, rinsed
8 ounces sherry
4 cups cold water
5 black peppercorns
1 bay leaf

HALIBUT
2 pounds halibut cheeks or small chunks of halibut
1 teaspoon salt
$\frac{1}{4}$ teaspoon ground black pepper
2 tablespoons olive oil
1 medium leek, light green and white part, sliced thin
12 medium mushrooms, sliced
1 pound sunchokes, peeled and sliced thin

■ To make the broth, melt the butter over medium heat in a 2-quart saucepan. Add the onion and celery and cook until soft. Add the garlic and shrimp shells and cook until the shells turn pink. Add the sherry and cook for 2 minutes. Add the water, peppercorns, and bay leaf, bring to a slow simmer, and cook for 1 hour. Strain. Over low heat, simmer the strained stock until reduced to 2 cups. Set aside.

■ Preheat the oven to 350°F.

- To prepare the halibut, season the halibut cheeks with salt and pepper. Heat the olive oil in a large sauté pan over medium-high heat until the oil shimmers. Sear the halibut cheeks for 1 minute on each side, then add the leeks, mushrooms, and sunchokes. Gently stir to combine. Add the broth. Bring to a simmer, cover the pan and place in the oven. Braise for 15 minutes.

- Divide the halibut cheeks among 4 warm soup bowls. Check the vegetables and shrimp-sherry broth for seasoning and ladle into the 4 bowls.

- Note: Clam juice may be substituted for the shrimp shells and water in making the broth. Simply omit the shells and add 4 cups clam juice instead of the water.

Serves four

Wild Alaska Snapper with Stir-Fry Vegetable Curry and Quick Fried Noodles

Al Levinsohn, Alyeska Resort

Levinsohn learned some of his skills in Hong Kong and Thailand and thus some of his food has a bent toward fusion. This dish is a good example. Snapper, or rockfish, is a common catch. Although often overlooked because of the amount of salmon and halibut in the local fish store, Alaska rockfish is clean-tasting and firm.

¼ cup ground toasted jasmine rice

3 tablespoons vegetable oil

4 Alaska snapper fillets (6 ounces each) or other snapper

Salt and ground white pepper

1 to 2 tablespoons red curry paste, depending on heat desired

2 tablespoons vegetable oil

1 cup diced Japanese eggplant

4 lime leaves

1 cup julienned carrots

½ cup julienned red onion

⅓ cup julienned red bell pepper

⅓ cup julienned yellow bell pepper

⅓ cup julienned green bell pepper

¼ cup Fish Stock (page 200) or Chicken Stock (page 197)

¾ cup coconut milk

1 cup bean sprouts

½ cup julienned snow peas

½ cup julienned green onion

½ cup Thai basil, shredded

¼ cup cilantro, chopped

2 cups fried vermicelli or bean thread noodles

Cilantro leaves

- Place the jasmine rice in a dry sauté pan and toast over high heat, moving the rice constantly until it is a medium brown color. Remove from the pan immediately to prevent burning. Let cool. Place in a coffee grinder and pulse until coarsely ground. Set aside.

- Preheat the oven to 400°F.

■ Heat 1 tablespoon of the vegetable oil in a 2-quart sauté pan over medium heat. Season the snapper fillets with salt and pepper. Quickly sear the fillets on both sides to medium rare, dust generously on all sides with ground toasted rice, and place, skin side down, on a baking tray. Dissolve the curry paste in the remaining 2 tablespoons vegetable oil. Heat the mixture until hot, then add the eggplant, lime leaves, and carrots. Sauté for 1 minute. Add the red onions and peppers. Sauté until just heated through.

■ Place fillets in the oven for 5 to 8 minutes, or until just done.

■ While the fillets are in the oven, add the stock to the eggplant mixture and bring to a slow boil. Add the coconut milk and return to a boil. Add the bean sprouts, snow peas, green onions, basil, and cilantro, and remove from the heat.

■ Divide the vegetable curry mixture among 4 warm plates. Top the curry with the fried noodles. Place the fillets on top of the noodles. Dust the plates with any remaining ground rice. Garnish with cilantro leaves and serve.

Serves four

Grilled Kodiak Scallops with Roasted Red Pepper Sauce

Jens Nannestad, Southside Bistro

This dish is good with Polenta Fritters (page 170). The trick is to cook the scallops only until they are rare or medium-rare.

ROASTED RED PEPPER SAUCE
4 Roma tomatoes, cored
6 cloves garlic, peeled
½ jalapeño pepper, chopped
½ small red onion, chopped
1 tablespoon olive oil
1 roasted red pepper, peeled and seeded
4 teaspoons aged balsamic vinegar
½ teaspoon salt
1 pinch ground black pepper

SCALLOPS
1½ pounds Kodiak scallops or other sea scallops
Salt and pepper
1 recipe Polenta Fritters (page 170)

■ Preheat the oven to 400°F.

■ To make the sauce, combine the tomatoes, garlic, jalapeño, red onion, and olive oil in a heavy ovenproof pan. Roast in the oven until the tomato skin blackens and blisters, 45 to 60 minutes. Combine the tomato mixture with the red pepper, vinegar, salt, and pepper in a food processor. Process until smooth. Taste for salt and pepper.

■ Preheat the grill.

■ To prepare the scallops, season with salt and pepper. Grill until medium rare, about 1 minute on each side. Or use a sauté pan.

■ Serve the scallops on a bed of roasted pepper sauce with the polenta fritters.

Serves four

Halibut Caddy Ganty

David and JoAnn Lesh, Gustavus Inn

This is the inn's most frequently requested recipe. Also called Halibut Olympia, it is on many menus throughout Alaska. Caddy Ganty was the wife of Pros Ganty, who was one of the founders of Pelican Cold Storage in Pelican, Alaska, in the 1920s. The town was named after his fish packer, called the Pelican. Many believe this is the original recipe, although it hasn't been verified.

> 1½ pounds halibut fillet
> Salt
> White wine
> Sourdough bread crumbs
> Butter
> 1½ cups sour cream
> ¾ cup mayonnaise
> ¾ cup onion, finely chopped
> Paprika

- Preheat the oven to 350°F.

- Skin the halibut fillet and cut it into pieces about 1 inch thick by 3 inches square. Place the halibut in a bowl, lightly salting and pouring the wine over each layer until the fish is all in. Cover and refrigerate for 2 hours.

- Drain the halibut and pat dry with a paper towel. Toss the halibut pieces in bread crumbs to coat and place them in a single layer in a lightly buttered baking dish that can be brought to the table. Mix the sour cream, mayonnaise, and onion and spread thickly on top of the fillets, smoothing out to the edges so the fish is covered completely. Sprinkle the top with paprika.

- Bake for 20 to 30 minutes, or until light brown and bubbly and the fish is just done. Serve right away.

> Serves four

Halibut Baked in Macadamia Nuts with Coconut Curry and Mango Chutney

Jack Amon, Marx Bros. Cafe

This Thai-influenced dish might be Amon's most famous recipe. He receives numerous requests for it. The fish is sturdy enough to stand up to the flavors of a variety of ingredients and takes well to the subtle Thai spicing.

RED CURRY PASTE

3 dried red Thai chiles
1 small onion, chopped
½ teaspoon fresh ground black pepper
1 teaspoon ground cumin
1½ teaspoons ground coriander
1 tablespoon chopped cilantro
½ teaspoon salt
1 tablespoon chopped lemongrass
1 clove garlic, chopped
1 teaspoon *kapi* (dried shrimp paste, available at Asian markets)
1 teaspoon vegetable oil
½ teaspoon turmeric
1 teaspoon paprika

HALIBUT

¾ cup flour
1 cup macadamia nuts
1½ pounds halibut fillet, skinned and cut into 4 equal portions
Salt and pepper
2 eggs, beaten with 2 tablespoons water
Vegetable oil spray
Pinch of cayenne
4 tablespoons (½ stick) butter, melted

PRESENTATION
2 tablespoons peanut oil
3 cups coconut milk
Mango Chutney (page 81)

■ To make the red curry paste, remove the stems from the chiles but keep the seeds in if you want the paste to be as hot as it is in Thailand. Break the chiles into pieces; put in a blender or food processor together with the remaining ingredients. Blend to a smooth paste, stopping frequently to scrape down sides of bowl. It may be necessary to add a tablespoon of water or extra oil. Set aside.

■ Preheat the oven to 375°F.

■ To prepare the halibut, place the flour on a plate. Chop the nuts in a food processor, then with a knife by hand until there are no large pieces. Place on another large plate.

■ About 15 minutes before service, lightly season each fillet with salt and pepper. Dredge the fillets in the flour on both sides and shake off the excess. Dip both sides of the fillets in eggs, then directly into the nuts, pressing lightly. Lightly spray a baking sheet with vegetable oil spray or wipe lightly with vegetable oil. Place the fillets on the baking sheet so that they do not touch. Pour 1 tablespoon of butter on top of each fillet.

■ Bake for 10 to 15 minutes, depending on the thickness of the fillets.

■ While the halibut is cooking, prepare the curry sauce. Heat the peanut oil in a heavy saucepan. Add 1/4 cup red curry paste, reserving any left over for another use, and cook for 1 minute. Add the coconut milk and bring to a boil. Reduce by half. Keep warm.

■ When the halibut is done, divide the curry sauce among 4 plates. Place the halibut on top of the sauce and garnish with a quarter of the mango chutney.

Serves four

Mango Chutney

 ¼ teaspoon minced dried Thai chiles
 1 clove garlic
 1 tablespoon peeled and minced fresh ginger
 6 tablespoons rice vinegar
 2 tablespoons sugar
 1 large firm mango, peeled and diced
 1 tablespoon chopped cilantro

- Combine the chiles, garlic, and ginger in a blender or food processor with 1 tablespoon of the rice vinegar and process. Combine the chile mixture with the remaining vinegar and the sugar in small saucepan, bring to a boil, and reduce heat to a simmer for 5 minutes.

- Remove from the heat, add the mango and cilantro, and let cool.

 Serves four

Halibut in Macadamia Nuts with Thai Curry Sauce

Jennifer Jolis, Jennifer's

This is similar to Jack Amon's recipe but with a few different twists and an easier curry method.

1½ pounds halibut fillet, skinned and cut into 4 equal portions
¾ cup flour
1 cup macadamia nuts
Salt and pepper
2 eggs, beaten
Vegetable oil spray
4 tablespoons (½ stick) butter, melted

THAI CURRY SAUCE
1 tablespoon peanut oil
1 tablespoon minced lemongrass
1½ tablespoons Thai red curry paste
2 cups coconut milk
Pinch of salt

■ Preheat the oven to 400°F.

■ To prepare the halibut, place the flour on a plate. Chop the nuts in a food processor, then with a knife by hand until there are no large pieces. Place on another large plate.

■ About 15 minutes before serving, lightly season each fillet with salt and pepper. Dredge the fillets through the flour on both sides and shake off any excess. Dip both sides of the fillets in the eggs, then directly into the nuts, pressing lightly. Lightly spray a baking sheet with vegetable oil spray or wipe lightly with vegetable oil. Place fillets on the baking sheet so that they do not touch. Drizzle each fillet with 1 tablespoon butter.

■ Bake for 10 to 15 minutes depending on the thickness of the fillets.

- Meanwhile, prepare the Thai curry sauce. Heat the oil in a medium saucepan. Add the lemongrass and curry paste and cook over medium heat for 1 minute. Add the coconut milk, raise the heat and bring to a simmer, and mix well. Reduce heat just to maintain the simmer. Reduce the sauce by one fourth. Adjust the flavor with salt.

- Put 3 tablespoons of sauce on a plate, top with cooked halibut, and serve.

Serves four

Hazelnut-Crusted Halibut with Citrus-Thyme Cream

Elizabeth King, Southside Bistro

This is a great springtime recipe. It goes well with Fiddlehead and Wild Mushroom Relish (page 176).

CITRUS-THYME CREAM
1 orange, zest and juice
1 lemon, zest and juice
1 shallot, minced
½ cup dry white wine
1 teaspoon white peppercorns
1¼ cups heavy cream
2 teaspoons chopped fresh thyme
3 tablespoons butter, cut into 4 pieces
Salt to taste

HALIBUT
½ cup raw hazelnuts
½ cup panko (Japanese bread crumbs, available in Asian grocery stores and some supermarkets)
2 teaspoons Italian parsley leaves
Salt and pepper
4 halibut fillets (6 ounces each)
1 egg, beaten
Olive oil, for frying

■ To make the citrus-thyme cream, combine the orange and lemon juices (reserve zests for later), shallot, wine, and peppercorns in a medium nonreactive saucepan over high heat. Bring to a low boil and reduce by two thirds. Strain, then return to the saucepan. Add the cream and bring to a simmer over medium heat. Adjust the heat to maintain a bare simmer so that the cream does not scorch. Simmer until the sauce is reduced by one third.

■ Remove from the heat and add the thyme. Whip in the butter, one piece at a time, until melted and well incorporated. Adjust seasoning. Fold in orange and lemon zests. Hold at room temperature; do not reheat.

■ Preheat the oven to 400°F.

- To prepare the halibut, put the hazelnuts, panko, parsley, and a pinch of salt and pepper in a food processor. Process until most of the hazelnuts are very small, with just a few larger pieces.

- Season the fillets lightly with salt and pepper. Dip the presentation side of a fillet into the beaten egg, then press firmly into the nut mixture. Repeat with remaining fillets.

- In an overproof skillet large enough to hold all the fillets, pour enough olive oil to cover the bottom by ⅛ inch. Heat the oil over medium-high heat until it shimmers. Add the fillets, nut side down. Cook until the nuts get to be an even light golden brown. Gently turn the fillets over. Place the pan in the oven and roast until the fish is just cooked through; it should be very moist. Serve right away with the citrus-thyme cream.

Serves four

Herb-Crusted Halibut

Farrokh Larijani, Glacier BrewHouse

This dish is one of the workhorses at Glacier BrewHouse. During the summer, they sell more than a thousand orders a month.

CILANTRO OIL
½ cup olive oil
¼ cup cilantro

HALIBUT
4 halibut fillets, skin off (6 ounces each)
¾ teaspoon kosher salt
¼ teaspoon ground black pepper
¼ cup Basil Pesto (page 87)
½ cup fresh bread crumbs

PRESENTATION
6 cups baby lettuce mix
1¼ cups Roasted Tomato Vinaigrette (page 189)
4 teaspoons Cilantro Oil (recipe above)

■ To make the cilantro oil, purée the oil and cilantro in a blender. Set aside ¼ cup and reserve remaining oil to garnish Southwestern dishes or as a base for a salad dressing.

■ Preheat the oven to 500°F.

■ To prepare the halibut, season the underneath side of the fillets with salt and pepper. Turn over and top each fillet with 1 tablespoon of the basil pesto. Divide the bread crumbs among the fillets and press them down lightly onto the fish. Place fillets in a roasting pan large enough to hold them without crowding. Roast the fish until just done. (Chef Larijani suggests cooking fish until they register 120°F on an instant-read thermometer.)

■ Toss the lettuce with ¼ cup of the vinaigrette. Place the dressed lettuce on 1 side of a dinner plate and top with the fillet. Spoon the remainder of the vinaigrette on the other side of the plate. Drizzle with cilantro oil and serve.

Serves four

Basil Pesto

1 cup chopped basil
¼ cup grated parmesan
1 tablespoon minced garlic
¼ cup walnuts, toasted
½ cup olive oil
1¼ teaspoons salt
¼ teaspoon ground black pepper

■ Put the basil, parmesan, garlic, and walnuts in a blender or food processor. With the motor running on medium speed, add the olive oil in a thin, steady stream. Season with salt and pepper. Refrigerate leftover pesto for a later use.

Makes 1¼ cups

Miso-Glazed Salmon with Corn Dumplings and Lemongrass-Wasabi Broth

Kirk McLean, Fiddlehead Restaurant and Bakery

Because of Japan's relative proximity and the large number of Japanese tourists, Japanese influences show up on Alaska menus. Fresh corn really makes this dish, but you may substitute frozen if it is out of season.

CORN DUMPLINGS

2 ears of corn

1 tablespoon vegetable oil

¼ cup diced onion

1 teaspoon minced garlic

½ teaspoon chopped fresh thyme

2 small red potatoes, cooked, peeled, and diced

12 gyoza wrappers (wonton wrappers)

LEMONGRASS-WASABI BROTH

2 stalks lemongrass

1 cup sake

1 cup Fish Stock (page 200)

½ teaspoon prepared wasabi

½ teaspoon minced fresh ginger

2 cloves garlic, minced

Salt and ground black pepper

SALMON

1 cup Fish Stock (page 200) or clam juice

3 tablespoons miso

4 salmon fillets (6 ounces each)

■ To make the corn dumplings, cut the corn kernels from the cob. Heat the oil in a skillet over medium-high heat until it shimmers. Add the corn and sauté until the kernels begin to brown. Add the onion and continue to cook until it begins to soften. Add the garlic and thyme and cook, stirring, for 1 minute. Remove from the heat. Add the diced potatoes and let the mixture cool.

- Lay out the gyoza wrappers on a cutting board. Spoon an equal amount of the corn mixture onto the center of each. Fold the wrapper over and press firmly to seal. Refrigerate.

- To make the lemongrass-wasabi broth, crush the lemongrass with a hammer, then chop. Combine the lemongrass, sake, fish stock, wasabi, ginger, and garlic in a medium saucepan and bring to a slow simmer. Cook for 30 minutes. Strain and set aside. Keep warm.

- To prepare the salmon, bring the stock to a simmer. Add the miso and dissolve. Cook for 5 minutes. Cool, then refrigerate.

- When the miso broth is completely cold, add the salmon and marinate for 2 to 3 hours.

- Prepare the grill.

- Bring a large saucepan with 8 cups of salted water to a boil.

- Grill the salmon on both sides until just done, basting continuously with the miso marinade.

- Simmer the dumplings in boiling water for 3 minutes. Remove with a slotted spoon.

- Place a salmon fillet in each of 4 large, warm soup bowls. Surround each fillet with 3 dumplings. Gently pour some hot broth over. Serve immediately.

Serves four

Whole-Grain Mustard–Crusted Halibut with Citrus Butter Sauce

Kirk McLean, Fiddlehead Restaurant and Bakery

This is a simple, rich way to prepare halibut. Other firm white fish may be substituted.

CITRUS BUTTER SAUCE
2 cups dry white wine
Zest of 1 orange
Zest of 1 lemon
Zest of 1 lime
2 tablespoons heavy cream
8 ounces (2 sticks) salted butter, cut into 1-tablespoon pieces
Salt

HALIBUT
1 cup whole-grain prepared mustard
2 tablespoons Dijon mustard
2 tablespoons minced garlic
¼ cup dry white wine
1½ pounds halibut fillet

- To make the citrus butter sauce, bring the wine and citrus zests to a boil in a medium saucepan, then lower the heat until the wine mixture simmers. Reduce wine mixture by half. Add the cream and simmer for 5 minutes. Remove the saucepan from the heat and whip in the butter, one piece at a time, until it is all incorporated. Taste the sauce and add salt to taste. Hold at room temperature; do not reheat.

- Preheat the oven to 400°F.

- To prepare the halibut, combine the whole-grain and Dijon mustard, garlic, and wine. Trim the skin from the halibut and cut the fish into 4 equal fillets. Place the fillets in a small roasting pan without crowding. Spread an equal amount of the mustard mixture evenly on top of each fillet. Cover and let rest for 15 minutes.

- Roast the halibut until just done, about 8 to 10 minutes. Place the fillets on 4 warm plates, dress with the reserved sauce, and serve.

    Serves four

Pepper-Crusted Sashimi Ahi with Cucumber Coulis and Wasabi Vinaigrette

Steve Gadbois, Sacks Cafe

The seared sashimi trend did not skip Alaska. Since Alaskans have a palate for fish and Asian flavors, it was sure to catch on. A hot sauté pan and excellent, best-quality tuna are key to this dish.

1 cup coarsely chopped peeled and seeded cucumber
1 cup plain yogurt
½ teaspoon crushed red pepper
1 teaspoon salt
2 tablespoons wasabi powder
2 tablespoons water
½ cup tamari
2 tablespoons sesame oil
1 pound sushi grade tuna
2 tablespoons Szechuan peppercorns
4 tablespoons vegetable oil
3 heads of baby bok choy, roughly chopped
½ cup bean sprouts
4 cups cooked jasmine rice
Daikon sprouts, for garnish

- Place the cucumber, yogurt, red pepper, and salt in a food processor and process until smooth. Refrigerate.

- Combine the wasabi powder and water in a small bowl and mix to a paste. Blend in the tamari. Whisk in the sesame oil in a thin, steady stream. Taste to determine if salt is needed. Set aside.

- Trim the tuna, then portion it into 4 equal pieces. Grind the peppercorns until coarse and dust the outside of each piece of tuna with them. Add 2 tablespoons of the vegetable oil to a heavy skillet and place over medium-high heat until the oil shimmers. Sear each side of the tuna for 30 seconds. Keep warm.

- Add the remaining vegetable oil to the skillet and briefly sauté the bok choy and bean sprouts together. Add the rice and heat through.

- Divide the cucumber coulis equally among 4 plates. Place one fourth of the rice-vegetable mixture on top of the coulis. Top with tuna. Drizzle wasabi vinaigrette around the outside of the plate, sprinkle daikon sprouts on top for garnish, and serve.

Serves four

How to Fillet a Salmon

Whether you catch your own salmon or buy a whole, gutted fish at the store, you'll need to know how to fillet it. The key to clean fillets with little waste is the right knife. A fillet knife with a long, thin blade is best. It must be absolutely sharp or you will end up pulverizing the flesh.

Here's how to fillet:

- If your fish is already gutted, as it should be from the fishmonger, make sure you rinse it well to remove any remaining blood.

- Hold the salmon by the tail with one hand (a towel can sometimes help).

- If the head is still attached, saw it off just behind the gills.

- Start at the backbone and cut steadily along one side of the fish from tail to head, exposing the bone.

- Start at the tail again and, keeping the knife parallel with the fish, slice the meat from the ribs. You can slowly pull the fillet away from the ribs as you cut.

- Flip the fish over and repeat.

- At this point, you should be able to lift the fish by the backbone and slice it away from the meat.

- Cut off the tail, trim off the belly skin and any rough edges of the meat and you should have two beautiful fillets.

Pepper-Crusted Salmon with King Crab–Infused Mashed Potatoes and Shellfish Stock

Jack Amon, Marx Bros. Cafe

This sophisticated dish uses all parts of the King crab legs and pairs salmon with flavored mashed potatoes, a bistro-style trend just starting to get popular in Alaska.

SHELLFISH BUTTER
8 ounces lobster or crab shells
8 ounces (2 sticks) unsalted butter

POTATOES
2 pounds King crab legs, in shell
1½ pounds Yukon Gold potatoes, peeled and sliced
3 tablespoons unsalted butter, at room temperature
⅓ cup heavy cream, warmed
Salt and ground white pepper
3 tablespoons finely chopped chives

SALMON
4 salmon fillets (6 ounces each)
¾ cup peppercorns, crushed
¼ cup Clarified Butter (page 205) or vegetable oil
2 cups Shellfish Stock (page 201)
2 leeks, white parts only, cut into thin strips, fried

■ Preheat the oven to 400°F.

■ To prepare the shellfish butter, roast the shells until crisp and dry. Crush the shells with a hammer or food processor. Place the shells and butter in a heavy medium saucepan over low heat. When the butter is melted, continue to cook over low heat for 45 minutes. Skim the foam. Strain the butter, discarding the shells, and refrigerate.

■ Shell the crab legs. Dice the meat and set aside. Set aside the shells.

■ To prepare the potatoes, place them in a large, heavy pot and cover with salted water. Bring to a boil, then reduce to a simmer. Cook until the potatoes are soft. Drain. Transfer the potatoes to a mixing bowl and beat in 3 tablespoons of the shellfish butter, the unsalted butter, and the cream. Season with salt and pepper. Stir in the chives and reserved crabmeat. Keep warm.

■ To prepare the salmon, lightly coat the presentation side of the fillets with the crushed pepper. Heat the clarified butter or oil in a heavy ovenproof skillet over medium-high heat until very hot. Place the salmon fillets in the skillet, pepper side down, and cook for 5 to 7 minutes. Place the skillet in the oven, without turning the fish over, and cook for 7 to 10 minutes more, or until the salmon is just done.

■ Divide the potatoes among 4 large pasta bowls. Place a salmon fillet, pepper side up, on top of the potatoes. Ladle shellfish stock over each portion, garnish with fried leeks, and serve.

Serves four

Peppered Halibut with Ginger Butter

Al Levinsohn, Alyeska Resort

This dish also works well on a grill.

> 8 tablespoons (1 stick) butter
> 2 teaspoon minced fresh ginger
> 1 teaspoon plus 1 tablespoon coarsely cracked black pepper
> 1 teaspoon minced garlic
> Salt
> 4 Alaska halibut fillets (5 ounces each)
> Kosher salt
> 2 tablespoons olive oil

- Place the butter, ginger, 1 teaspoon of the pepper, and garlic in a food processor or mixer. Process or whip until all ingredients are incorporated. Season with salt. Hold at room temperature.

- Season each fillet with the remaining 1 tablespoon pepper, pressing the pepper firmly into the flesh of the fish. Season each fillet with kosher salt.

- Add the olive oil to a large skillet and heat over medium-high heat until the oil shimmers. Pan-sear the halibut, skin side up, until the fish forms a golden crust. Turn the fish over and cook until it is firm to the touch and just cooked through.

- Place the fillets on warm plates and top each with an equal amount of the reserved ginger butter.

> Serves four

Cold Poached Salmon with Mint Mayonnaise

David and JoAnn Lesh, Gustavus Inn

Arrange poached salmon fillets on lettuce leaves on a fish platter. Decorate with baby garden vegetables and garnish with lemon wedges, edible flowers, and herb leaves. Leave a spot on the platter for a small ramekin of mint mayonnaise.

MINT MAYONNAISE
1 egg
2 tablespoons plus ¾ cup vegetable oil
2 tablespoons vinegar
15 fresh mint leaves, or more to taste
½ teaspoon salt

SALMON
1 medium onion, thinly sliced
1 carrot, thinly sliced
1 stalk celery, thinly sliced
10 black peppercorns, cracked
6 parsley stems
½ cup dry white wine
2 quarts cold water
1 lemon, halved
1½ pounds Alaska salmon fillet, skin off

GARNISH
Baby garden vegetables, such as carrots, radish roses, and snow peas
Lemon wedges, edible flowers, parsley and mint leaves

■ Place the egg, 2 tablespoons oil, vinegar, mint leaves, and salt in a blender and mix on high speed for 1 minute. Reduce the speed to slow, then add the remaining ¾ cup oil in a thin, steady stream. Taste and adjust the seasoning. Refrigerate.

■ Combine the onion, carrot, celery, peppercorns, parsley stems, wine, and water in a medium roasting pan or rectangular cake pan. Place on top of the stove and bring to a boil. Reduce the heat to very low and squeeze the lemon into the water. Toss the lemon in. When the poaching liquid is steaming, add the salmon. (It is very important that the liquid is only steaming, not boiling or simmering. Poaching is a gentle process.) Allow the salmon to just cook through, about 10 minutes. Remove. Refrigerate until well chilled.

■ Transfer the fish to a platter and decorate with baby garden vegetables, lemon wedges, edible flowers, herb leaves, and a small ramekin of mint mayonnaise.

Serves four

Porcini and Arborio-Crusted Halibut with Kalamata-Artichoke Relish

Farrokh Larijani, Glacier BrewHouse

The olive-artichoke relish gives this dish a California cuisine twist. Rice flour adds a light touch to the sautéed halibut. The relish is courtesy of Glacier BrewHouse Chef Patio Nelson.

KALAMATA-ARTICHOKE RELISH
3 ounces marinated artichoke hearts, cut into ½-inch chunks
2 tablespoons roughly chopped Kalamata olives
2 tablespoons diced (¼ inch) roasted red onion
2 tablespoons diced (¼ inch) roasted red bell pepper
2 tablespoons diced (¼ inch) roasted green bell pepper
⅓ cup roughly chopped cilantro
¼ cup Roasted Roma Tomatoes (page 190)
2 tablespoons balsamic thyme vinaigrette

BALSAMIC THYME VINAIGRETTE
¼ cup white balsamic vinegar
2 cloves garlic
¾ teaspoon fresh thyme, chopped
¼ teaspoon coarsely ground black pepper
¼ cup olive oil

HALIBUT
1½ pounds halibut fillet
¼ teaspoon black pepper
½ teaspoon kosher salt
2 tablespoons flour
3 egg whites
½ cup Arborio flour (see Note)
½ cup rice flour
2 tablespoons porcini mushroom powder
6 tablespoons olive oil

- To make the kalamata-artichoke relish, mix all the ingredients together. Set aside.

- To make the balsamic thyme vinaigrette, whisk together the vinegar, garlic, thyme, and pepper. Add the oil in a thin, steady stream, whisking constantly. Set aside.

- Preheat the oven to 350°F.

- To prepare the halibut, cut the fish into 4 equal fillets. Season the fillets with pepper and salt. Dredge the fillets in flour, shaking off the excess. Dip the fillets in the egg whites. Mix together the Arborio flour, rice flour, and mushroom powder. Dredge the fillets in the rice flour mixture.

- Heat the oil in a heavy ovenproof skillet until it shimmers. Sear the fillets on both sides. Transfer the pan to the oven and cook for about 10 minutes, or until just done. Drain on paper towels.

- Transfer the halibut to warmed plates, top each with 3 tablespoons of the relish. Drizzle 1½ tablespoons of vinaigrette around each fillet. Serve right away.

- Note: if Arborio flour is unavailable, use a total of 1 cup rice flour.

Serves four

Roasted Dungeness Crab with Pasta

Farrokh Larijani, Glacier BrewHouse

This dish is done in the wood-fired oven at the Glacier BrewHouse. You can get a similar effect in your home oven.

> 4 pounds Dungeness crab legs, scored
> ¼ cup chopped parsley
> ¼ cup chopped basil
> 3 tablespoon minced garlic
> 1 cup olive oil
> 1 tablespoon black pepper, cracked
> 1 teaspoon kosher salt
> Juice of 2 lemons
> 12 ounces dried pasta, such as linguine or spaghetti
> 4 lemon wedges
> 8 sprigs of Italian parsley

- Preheat the oven to 400°F.

- Bring 3 quarts of water to a boil in a large stockpot with 2 teaspoons of salt.

- Combine the crab, parsley, basil, garlic, olive oil, pepper, salt, and lemon juice. Toss well. Place the crab legs in a roasting pan and drizzle with mixture left in the bowl.

- Roast the crab until it is almost heated through, about 8 minutes. Watching closely, finish the crab under the broiler until the edges just start to char.

- While the crab is roasting, cook the pasta until al dente. Drain.

- Divide the pasta among 4 plates. Arrange the crab legs around the pasta and drizzle crab and pasta with the remaining oil mixture from the roasting pan. Garnish each plate with a lemon wedge and 2 sprigs of parsley and serve.

Serves four

Roasted Salmon with Sauce Verde

Farrokh Larijani, Glacier BrewHouse

The pungent Sauce Verde gives the salmon a serious kick. It can also be used as a dip for vegetables or even be tossed with pasta.

SAUCE VERDE
2 anchovy fillets
⅓ cup capers
1½ tablespoons minced garlic
2 cups parsley
2 tablespoons fresh lemon juice
½ teaspoon ground black pepper
¼ cup fresh basil
2 tablespoons fresh mint
1½ teaspoons fresh thyme
½ cup olive oil
Vegetable Stock (page 199)

SALMON
4 Alaska salmon fillets, skin on (6 ounces each)
1 teaspoon ground black pepper
¼ teaspoon granulated garlic
3 tablespoons chopped tarragon
3 tablespoons thinly sliced shallots
1 leek, white part, julienned
8 thin slices fresh lemon
Olive oil
½ cup Lemon Aïoli (page 194)

■ To make the sauce verde, place the anchovies, capers, garlic, parsley, lemon juice, pepper, basil, mint, and thyme in a blender. With the blender running, pour in the olive oil in a thin, steady stream. Add enough stock to bring the paste to sauce consistency.

■ Preheat the oven to 450°F.

■ With a sharp knife, pull the skin back from each fillet. Season with pepper and garlic. Place the tarragon, shallots, leek, and lemon slices on top. Put the skin back over the tarragon mixture. Place the fillets on an ovenproof pan and coat the salmon skin with olive oil.

■ Roast in the oven until just done. Put the fillets on hot plates and top with lemon aïoli. Drizzle each plate with $1/4$ cup of the sauce verde.

Serves four

Grilled Wild Alaska Salmon with Tomato-Arugula Salsa

Jens Nannestad, Southside Bistro

The secret of preparing great seafood is to not overcook it. The preferred salmon for this recipe would be the first run of the famous Copper River King salmon. However, any fresh salmon or other fresh broiler-friendly fish will certainly suit this recipe.

TOMATO-ARUGULA SALSA
8 Roma tomatoes, cored and diced small
¾ cup chopped arugula
1 shallot, finely chopped
2 cloves garlic, minced
2 tablespoons capers
3 tablespoons fresh lemon juice
¾ teaspoon salt
¼ teaspoon black pepper
1½ tablespoons olive oil

SALMON
1¾ pounds salmon fillet
½ cup Herb Olive Oil (page 104)
Kosher salt and pepper

- To make the salsa, combine all the ingredients and refrigerate.

- Preheat the grill.

- To prepare the salmon, skin, trim, and remove the pin bones from the salmon fillet. Divide into 4 equal portions. Brush the fish with the herb olive oil and season lightly with salt and pepper.

- Grill on a very hot grill until just done. Baste with more herb olive oil during the cooking.

- When done, place each piece of fish on a warm plate, top with one fourth of the salsa, and serve.

Serves four

Herb Olive Oil

⅓ cup olive oil
2 tablespoons basil
2 tablespoons parsley
2 teaspoons marjoram
1 teaspoon thyme

■ Purée the oil and herbs in a blender.

Makes ½ cup

Grilled Salmon with Balsamic Reduction and Tomato-Leek Relish

JoAnn Asher, Sacks Cafe

The reduction of vinegar adds a sharp-sweet note to the rich salmon. The smoky relish is a perfect foil.

TOMATO-LEEK RELISH

6 Roma tomatoes

1 leek, white part only, halved, sliced, and cleaned

2 teaspoons chopped garlic

1 teaspoon salt

1 teaspoon granulated sugar

2 tablespoons olive oil

SALMON

1½ pounds salmon fillet

24 ounces balsamic vinegar

3 tablespoons (packed) brown sugar

1 tablespoon Worcestershire sauce

½ teaspoon crushed red pepper

- Preheat the oven to 350°F.

- To make the relish, core and quarter the tomatoes. Add the leek, garlic, salt, sugar, and olive oil. Gently mix until combined. Place the tomato mixture in a baking pan or Pyrex dish. Roast for 20 minutes, or until the tomato skins start to wrinkle. Keep warm.

- To prepare the salmon, skin and trim the fillet, cut into 4 equal portions, and set aside.

- In a small saucepan, reduce the balsamic vinegar by two thirds, about 30 minutes.

- Add brown sugar, Worcestershire sauce and red pepper. Simmer 3 to 5 minutes, or until of syrup-like consistency. Remove from the heat and let rest 5 minutes before use. (This reduction keeps very well in the refrigerator. Bring it to room temperature before using.)

- Preheat the grill.

■ Grill the salmon for 5 to 10 minutes, or until just done. Place on a warm plate, drizzle with the balsamic reduction, and top with the relish.

Serves four

A Salmon Primer

To many cooks, Alaska is synonymous with salmon, and with good reason. Each year, nearly 200 million wild salmon are commercially harvested in Alaska. Hundreds of thousands more are taken by sport anglers or by Alaska Natives who use the fish to sustain them through the winter. Although five different species are harvested, three show up regularly in restaurants and in home kitchens: Kings (Chinooks), Silvers (Cohos), and Reds (Sockeyes).

Silvers are known as fine fighting fish. Reds are one of Alaska's favorite eating fish, and Kings, also prized, are the largest. A 120-pound King Salmon is thought to have spent about seven years in the ocean.

The superior flavor and firm, meaty flesh of wild salmon are worth searching for. Farm-raised salmon, often from the Atlantic Ocean, are pale and mushy in comparison. Wild Alaska salmon can sometimes be found at fish markets in the Lower 48, and Alaska fish companies will ship fresh salmon (see page 232). If you live on the West Coast, wild King salmon from the Pacific Northwest or the California coast is seasonally available and a reasonable alternative.

Scallops in Saffron and
Pernod Cream Sauce with Caviar

Jens Hansen, Jens' Restaurant and Bodega

Anise liqueur and saffron are a classic flavor combination. The sauce is delicate enough not to overpower the scallops. The caviar gives the dish an elegant touch.

> 24 sea scallops
> 2 tablespoons Clarified Butter (page 205)
> 2 ounces Pernod
> 1 cup Fish Stock (page 200) or clam juice
> ¼ teaspoon saffron threads
> 1 cup heavy cream
> 2 tablespoons butter
> 2 ounces beluga or other caviar

- Pan-fry the scallops in clarified butter in a smoking hot pan for 20 seconds on each side. Remove the scallops and keep warm; don't clean out the frying pan.

- Add the Pernod, fish stock, and saffron. Reduce the liquid to 6 tablespoons over high heat. Stir in the heavy cream and reduce to ½ cup. Remove the pan from the heat and whip in the butter.

- Divide the sauce among 4 plates. Place the scallops on the sauce and sprinkle caviar over the shellfish. Serve right away.

> Serves four

Sesame-Crusted Salmon with Miso Vinaigrette

Jack Amon, Marx Bros. Cafe

The crunch of the sesame seeds and the bright flavors of the miso sauce make for a stunning combination.

MISO VINAIGRETTE

2½ tablespoons white miso

2 tablespoons fresh lemon juice

1 tablespoon Thai sweet chile sauce

2 tablespoons rice wine vinegar

1½ teaspoons finely chopped garlic

1½ teaspoons finely chopped shallot

3 tablespoons peeled and finely chopped fresh ginger

2 tablespoons soy sauce

1 tablespoon dry sherry or mirin

1 teaspoon sugar

1 cup peanut oil

¼ cup sesame oil

3 green onions, sliced very thin

SALMON

1½ pounds salmon fillet

⅓ cup white sesame seeds

⅓ cup black sesame seeds

¼ cup vegetable oil

4 heads of baby bok choy, steamed

1 cup Miso Vinaigrette (recipe above)

6 ounces ogo or other seaweed (available at Asian markets and some seafood stores), steamed

■ To make the miso vinaigrette, put all the ingredients except the peanut and sesame oil and the green onions into a food processor and process until smooth. With the motor running, slowly add the oils. Remove the vinaigrette, add the green onions, and set aside.

■ Preheat the oven to 400°F.

- Skin, trim, and debone salmon, if not already done. Cut into 4 equal fillets.

- In a bowl, combine the white and black sesame seeds. Press the presentation side of each fillet into the seeds.

- Heat the oil in a heavy ovenproof skillet until it shimmers. Sear the sesame-crusted side of the salmon about 3 minutes or until the white seeds are golden. Turn the fillets to other side. Transfer the pan to the oven and cook for about 10 minutes, or until just done. Drain on paper towels.

- Transfer the salmon to 4 warmed plates, top each with $1/4$ cup of vinaigrette, reserving any leftover vinaigrette for another use. Garnish with the steamed bok choy and seaweed and serve.

Serves four

Sesame Salmon Cakes with Soy-Ginger Glaze

Elizabeth King, Southside Bistro

The pronounced flavor of wild salmon is preferred for this recipe, but farmed Atlantic salmon will do in a pinch.

SALMON CAKES

20 ounces raw Alaska salmon

⅓ cup minced red onion

⅓ cup minced celery

¾ cup minced red bell pepper

2 green onions, thinly sliced

½ jalapeño, minced

¼ cup finely chopped cilantro

3 teaspoons sesame oil

1¾ teaspoons kosher salt

Ground black pepper

3 tablespoons soy sauce

3 tablespoons heavy cream

2 tablespoons flour

1 egg white

1 tablespoon fresh lemon juice

Vegetable oil

¼ cup black sesame seeds

¼ cup white sesame seeds

¼ cup flour

SOY-GINGER GLAZE

¾ cup soy sauce

6 tablespoons rice wine vinegar

10 tablespoons (packed) brown sugar

1 tablespoon chopped fresh ginger

1 tablespoon cornstarch

1 tablespoon cold water

- Divide the salmon into 2 portions, one weighing 12 ounces, the other 8 ounces. Finely chop the 12-ounce portion. Roughly chop the 8-ounce portion. Keep separate.

- Combine the 12-ounce portion of finely chopped salmon, the red onion, celery, bell pepper, green onions, jalapeño, cilantro, $1\frac{1}{2}$ teaspoons of the sesame oil, 1 teaspoon of the salt, and $\frac{1}{4}$ teaspoon of pepper in a mixing bowl. Cover and refrigerate until chilled.

- Put the 8-ounce portion of roughly chopped salmon, the soy sauce, cream, flour, egg white, lemon juice, the remaining $1\frac{1}{2}$ teaspoons of sesame oil, the remaining $\frac{3}{4}$ teaspoon salt, and a pinch of pepper in a food processor. Purée until smooth, scraping down the sides of the bowl during the process. Remove to a large bowl.

- Fold in the finely chopped salmon mixture. Make a small patty, pan-fry in a small amount of oil. Taste for seasoning. Adjust with more salt and/or pepper to taste. Make another test patty if necessary. Shape into 8 patties for a main course or 16 for appetizers. Cover and refrigerate for 4 hours.

- Meanwhile, mix together the black and white sesame seeds and flour. Set aside.

- Shortly before serving, prepare the soy-ginger glaze. Combine the soy sauce, vinegar, brown sugar, and ginger in a small saucepan. Bring to a simmer. Mix the cornstarch and water in a teacup until well combined. Whisk the cornstarch mixture into the soy sauce mixture. Simmer 5 minutes, then strain.

- To serve, dredge the patties in the sesame-seed mixture. Pan-fry in vegetable oil on each side until golden, about 4 to 5 minutes. Drain on paper towels and serve with the soy-ginger glaze. Discard any remaining sesame seed mixture.

Serves four as a main course or eight as an appetizer

Alaska Spot Shrimp and Smoked Gouda Polenta Tart with Avocado Salsa

Toby Ramey, Sacks Cafe

Alaska spot shrimp are sweet and plump, and are sometimes sold with a pocket of orange roe in their bellies. Tiger or other shrimp can be substituted.

AVOCADO SALSA
4 Roma tomatoes, cored and diced
½ red onion, finely diced
1 jalapeño, finely diced, seeded if you like it mild
2 avocados, diced
Juice of ½ lime
1½ teaspoons minced garlic
¼ cup chopped cilantro
Salt and ground black pepper

TART
2 teaspoons olive oil
½ teaspoon ground cumin
½ teaspoon granulated garlic
½ teaspoon ancho chile powder
½ teaspoon dried thyme
1½ pounds Alaska spot shrimp or size 26/30 tiger shrimp, peeled and deveined
2¼ cups water
2 tablespoons butter
1 teaspoon kosher salt
½ cup polenta
½ cup yellow cornmeal
½ cup grated smoked gouda
Nonstick vegetable oil spray

■ To make the avocado salsa, mix together the tomatoes, onion, jalapeño, avocados, lime juice, and garlic and season with salt and pepper. Set aside.

■ Preheat the oven to 325°F.

- To make the tart, combine the olive oil, cumin, garlic, chile powder, and thyme in a large bowl. Add the shrimp and toss to coat. Refrigerate.

- Combine the water, butter, and salt in a large saucepan and bring to a boil. Mix together the polenta and cornmeal and add the mixture to the boiling water. Whisk until smooth with no lumps. Over low heat, stir the polenta with a wooden spoon for 3 minutes. Remove from the heat. Add gouda and stir until melted. The polenta should be thick, but spreadable.

- Spray a 9-inch tart pan (with a removable bottom) with nonstick vegetable oil spray. Arrange the shrimp evenly around the bottom of the tart pan, leaving a 1/2-inch border. Starting at the outside of the tart pan, use a rubber spatula to fill the border between the pan and the shrimp with the polenta mixture. Spread the remaining polenta mixture over the shrimp and smooth it to a uniform thickness. Bake for 10 minutes, or until polenta is firm, not crisp. Invert onto a cutting board and cut into 6 wedges.

- Place on warm plates, garnish with salsa and serve.

Serves six

Ale-Poached Shrimp with Warm Belly Cocktail Sauce

Mark Linden, Glacial Reflections Catering

Alaska spot shrimp, sometimes called Alaska lobster, are available between April and October, though they can be hard to find. Their sweet taste makes them worth the search. If they are unavailable, use fresh or frozen large shrimp, size 16/20. The sauce, as the name implies, is spicy.

WARM BELLY COCKTAIL SAUCE

1 cup ketchup

⅓ cup chile sauce

1 jalapeño, seeded and minced

1 teaspoon minced garlic

½ cup minced red onion

¼ cup chopped cilantro

Juice of 1 lime

¼ cup horseradish, or to taste

½ teaspoon Tabasco

½ teaspoon Worcestershire sauce

Salt and pepper

SHRIMP

1 teaspoon whole fennel seeds

1 teaspoon mustard seed

1 teaspoon black peppercorns

1 teaspoon whole allspice

½ teaspoon whole cloves

¼ cup olive oil

½ red onion, peeled and chopped

1 jalapeño, chopped

2 cloves garlic, peeled and mashed

Zest of 1 orange

1 teaspoon crushed red pepper

48 ounces Alaska amber ale or other high-quality ale

24 large spot or side-striped shrimp, unpeeled

- To make the cocktail sauce, combine all the ingredients, adjust the seasonings, and refrigerate.

- Place a medium-size heavy-gauge saucepan over medium-low heat. Add fennel seeds, mustard, peppercorns, allspice, and cloves. Stir until lightly toasted and an aroma rises. Add the olive oil and increase the heat to medium. When the oil shimmers, add the red onion, and jalapeño. Cook, stirring, for 5 minutes. Add the garlic, orange zest, red pepper, and ale. Increase the heat and stir until the liquid comes to a simmer. Cook for 15 minutes to marry the flavors.

- Add the shrimp and immediately reduce the heat until the liquid just steams. Poach the shrimp until just cooked, about 8 to 10 minutes. Remove the shrimp and refrigerate until chilled. Peel the shrimp, leaving the tail, and serve with the cocktail sauce.

Serves four

Sonoran Seafood Stew

Sean Maryott, The Homestead

Maryott takes his inspiration from the Sonoran influence prevalent in his home state of Arizona.

1½ pounds steamer clams, scrubbed
1 tablespoon minced garlic
⅓ cup minced parsley
1 cup sauvignon blanc wine
¾ pound fresh mussels, scrubbed and debearded
1 tablespoon butter
2 tablespoons Cilantro Pesto (page 67)
1 tablespoon chipotle chile paste
¼ cup green onions, thinly sliced
¼ cup diced red onions
¼ cup thinly sliced mushrooms
¼ cup roasted, peeled, and chopped pasilla chile
2 cups diced Roma tomatoes
4 ounces halibut, large chunks
4 ounces salmon, large chunks
4 ounces bay scallops or quartered sea scallops
16 jumbo prawns, peeled and deveined
2 cups Fish Stock (page 200)
12 shucked oysters
8 ounces fresh squid, cleaned and roughly chopped
2 cups cooked rice

■ Combine the clams, garlic, parsley, and wine in a large soup pot and bring to a simmer. Cover and cook for 5 minutes. Discard any unopened clams. Add the mussels, butter, pesto, chipotle chile paste, green onions, red onions, mushrooms, pasilla chile, tomatoes, halibut, salmon, scallops, prawns, and stock. Cook until the seafood begins to glaze and mussels open. Discard any unopened mussels. Add the oysters and squid, cover and bring to a simmer. Turn off the heat.

■ Divide the rice among 4 large soup bowls. Ladle the stew over and serve.

Serves four

Roulade of Yellowfin Tuna Tartare

Jens Hansen, Jens' Restaurant and Bodega

The quality of fish in Alaska—even fish shipped in—is usually so good that eating it raw never raises an eyebrow. Make sure the fish you buy is fresh and clean-smelling.

> 2 pounds sushi grade yellowfin (ahi) tuna, coarsely chopped
> 1 green mango, peeled and chopped
> 2 tablespoons ketchup
> 1 teaspoon hot sesame oil
> 1 tablespoon Thai fish sauce
> 6 green onions, thinly sliced
> 1 tablespoon whole cumin seeds, toasted
> 3 tablespoons prepared wasabi
> 3 tablespoons peeled and grated fresh horseradish
> 2 English cucumbers
> Arugula leaves
> Smoked Alaska salmon caviar or other caviar (optional)
> Rose petals (optional)

- For the tartare filling, mix the tuna, mango, ketchup, hot sesame oil, Thai fish sauce, green onions, and cumin seeds in a large bowl. Refrigerate.

- In a small bowl, mix together the wasabi and horseradish. Set aside.

- Trim the ends from the cucumbers, then slice thin with a mandoline or similar slicer. Lightly brush 1 one side of each cucumber slice with the wasabi-horseradish mixture. Spread some tuna mixture on each cucumber slice. Roll the tuna-topped cucumber slices into rolls. Place on a pan and cover with plastic wrap. Freeze for 15 minutes.

- To serve, place arugula leaves on a chilled plate. Place the tartare rolls on the leaves. Dot with caviar and sprinkle rose petals over, if desired. Serve.

- Note: A mandoline is a manually operated slicer used in professional kitchens. Similar slicers made of plastic with stainless steel blades may be found in most kitchen shops.

> Serves six as a main course or twelve as an appetizer

Cioppino Shrimp with Shallot Risotto

Mark Linden, Glacial Reflections Catering

This is a great way to show off sweet Alaska spot prawns. However, you can use fresh or frozen large shrimp with a 16/20 count.

RISOTTO
2 tablespoons butter
¼ cup chopped shallots
4 ounces Arborio rice
3 cups Chicken Stock (page 197) or good-quality canned broth
Salt and ground white pepper
1 tablespoon truffle oil (optional)
¾ cup grated Parmigiano-Reggiano

SHRIMP
¼ cup olive oil
24 large spot or side-striped shrimp, peeled and deveined
2 ribs celery, cut into matchsticks
1 onion, cut into matchsticks
1 green pepper, cut into matchsticks
2 tablespoons minced garlic
¼ teaspoon saffron threads
2 cups Shellfish Stock (page 201)
½ cup tomato juice
¼ teaspoon crushed red pepper
½ cup sherry
1 tablespoon chopped tarragon leaves, stems reserved
½ tablespoon chopped basil leaves, stems reserved
1 teaspoon chopped fresh thyme, stems reserved
Salt and freshly ground black pepper

■ To make the risotto, melt the butter in a large saucepan over medium heat. Add the shallots and cook until golden. Add the rice and cook, stirring, for 3 minutes. Add the stock, a fourth at a time. Stir the rice continuously until each addition of stock is completely absorbed, 20 to 25 minutes. The rice should be cooked through, but still resistant to the bite. Remove from the heat and stir in the salt, pepper, truffle oil, and Parmigiano. Cover and keep warm. When it is time to serve, it may be necessary to add a bit more stock and cook over medium-low heat until thoroughly reheated.

■ For the shrimp, heat the olive oil in a large sauté pan over medium-high heat until it shimmers. Add the shrimp and sauté until just turns orange. Remove and set aside.

■ Add the celery, onion, and green pepper and sauté just until they begin to soften. Add the garlic and saffron and stir. Add the stock, tomato juice, red pepper, sherry, and herb stems. Bring to a simmer. Cook for 15 minutes. Remove the stems. Add the reserved shrimp and cook until just done.

■ Serve in large soup bowls over the risotto.

Serves four

Pan-Seared Beef Tenderloin with Pinot Noir Sauce and Mushroom Strudel

Farrokh Larijani, Glacier BrewHouse

Despite the abundance of seafood and the recent influence of cooking styles from Asia, California, and the Mediterranean, Alaskans love meat and potatoes. This recipe plays off that love of good beef but adds a little sophistication. Although this is labor-intensive, it is a great dish for a dinner party.

MUSHROOM STRUDEL

8 ounces portobello mushrooms

2 tablespoons butter

¼ cup diced (¼ inch) shallots

4 ounces medium button mushrooms, diced ¼ inch

2 teaspoons roughly chopped fresh oregano

1 teaspoon finely chopped rosemary

1 tablespoon roughly chopped basil

½ teaspoon kosher salt

½ teaspoon freshly ground black pepper

½ cup bread crumbs

4 egg roll wrappers

2 eggs, beaten

PINOT NOIR SAUCE

2 tablespoons olive oil

2 tablespoons chopped shallots

1 clove garlic, chopped

¼ cup chopped mushrooms

1 teaspoon chopped dried mushrooms

1 tablespoon chopped sun-dried tomatoes

1 tablespoon balsamic vinegar

½ cup pinot noir

1 bay leaf

1 sprig of thyme, chopped

1 tablespoon chopped basil

½ teaspoon freshly cracked black pepper

1½ cups demi-glace (available in specialty food shops)
1 teaspoon arrowroot
1 tablespoon water

TENDERLOIN
2 leeks, white and light green parts
Vegetable oil, for frying
20 ounces trimmed beef tenderloin
¾ teaspoon kosher salt
¼ teaspoon ground black pepper
4 tablespoons olive oil
4 tablespoons (½ stick) butter
20 spears fresh asparagus, steamed and kept warm

- To make the mushroom strudels, scrape the black gills off the portobello mushrooms with a spoon and remove the stems. Cut the mushroom caps and stems in ¼-inch dice. Heat the butter in a heavy skillet over medium-high heat until it foams. Add the shallots and portobello and button mushrooms. Sauté until cooked through, about 3 minutes. Remove from the heat, then stir in the oregano, rosemary, basil, salt, pepper, and bread crumbs. Cool to room temperature.

- Lay the egg roll wrappers out on a clean work surface. Spread the mushroom mixture evenly over the wrappers, leaving 1 inch free space on the wrapper on the edge away from you. Brush the free space with beaten egg. Beginning with the side near you, roll the wrapper, jelly-roll style, into a tight cylinder. Place the 4 cylinders on a greased baking tray, seam side down. Set aside.

- To make the pinot noir sauce, heat the olive oil in a heavy-gauge saucepan over medium-high heat until it shimmers. Add the shallots, garlic, and chopped mushrooms and sauté for 3 minutes. Add the dried mushrooms and sun-dried tomatoes and stir until incorporated. Add the balsamic vinegar and reduce by half.

- Add the pinot noir, bay leaf, thyme, basil, and pepper and reduce by half. Add the demi-glace and simmer for 10 minutes. Make a slurry of the arrowroot and water. Whipping constantly, add the slurry to the sauce in a steady stream. Simmer 5 minutes. Strain and keep warm.

- Preheat the oven to 400°F.

- Cut the leeks lengthwise into thin strips, then wash well. Pat dry. Heat the vegetable oil in a Dutch oven or deep-fat fryer to 350°F. Fry the leeks until golden brown, remove, and drain on paper towels. Set aside.

- Bake the strudels until golden brown. Remove and keep warm.

■ To prepare the tenderloin, cut it into 8 equal medallions. Season with salt and pepper. Heat the olive oil in a heavy sauté pan until it just begins to smoke. Sear the medallions on both sides until browned. Remove and keep warm. Turn the heat off on the stove. Discard the remaining oil in the pan. Add 1½ cups of the Pinot Noir Sauce, scraping any browned bits off the bottom of the pan with a wooden spoon. Swirl in the butter. Keep warm.

■ Cut the strudels in half diagonally. Stack the asparagus in the center of 4 large, warm dinner plates. Shingle 2 medallions on top of the asparagus. Arrange the 2 halves of a strudel next to the medallions. Drizzle a bit of sauce over the medallions and the remaining sauce all over the plates. Place a haystack of fried leeks on top of the medallions and serve.

Serves four

Chili Verde

Sean Maryott, The Homestead

All types of stew are at home in Alaska, where a hearty, warming bowl of anything tasty is welcome. This is an authentic, heavy-duty dish that is not exactly health food. Maryott says if you go to this much trouble, you might as well make enough for your favorite heart surgeon.

⅓ cup plus ½ cup olive oil
4 medium yellow onions, chopped
5 pounds boneless fresh pork shoulder roast
½ cup chopped fresh garlic
1 can (7 ounces) chipotle chiles in adobo sauce
2 tablespoons sea salt
½ cup tequila (optional)
2 cups Chicken Stock (page 197)
5 tomatillos, peeled and washed well
3 cups chopped roasted, peeled, and seeded green chiles
4 cups chopped tomatoes
4 red jalapeños, seeded and minced
1 cup fresh lime juice
1 cup chopped cilantro leaves
Sea salt

■ Preheat the oven to 350°F.

■ Heat the ⅓ cup olive oil in a Dutch oven or heavy roasting pan over medium-high heat until it shimmers. Add the onions and stir for 30 seconds. Add the pork shoulder and brown well on all sides. Add the garlic, chipotles, and salt. Stir for 1 to 2 minutes.

■ Add the tequila, if using, and stock to the pan. Stir to displace any brown bits on the bottom and sides of the pan. Cover the pan and cook in the oven for 1½ hours, or until the meat falls apart. Cool the meat and shred it into small pieces. Set the meat aside along with all of the ingredients left in the roasting pan.

■ Pierce the tomatillos with a fork and blister them over a burner, then purée them. Combine the tomatillos, green chiles, tomatoes, jalapeños, lime juice, and remaining ½ cup of olive oil in a large saucepan. Simmer over medium-high heat for 10 minutes. Add the reserved meat and ingredients left in the roasting pan.

Skim any fat. Bring to a simmer over medium-high heat and adjust the heat to maintain the simmer. Cook for 1 hour. Cool. Skim the fat.

■ Reheat to serve. Stir in the cilantro. Taste and adjust the seasoning and serve.

Serves 8

Moose

Moose doesn't show up on restaurant menus in Alaska, but the rich meat is as much a part of the state's table as salmon. Hunters take more than seven thousand moose each year. A mature male can weigh more than 1,500 pounds and cows half a ton. That breaks down to as much as 700 pounds of edible meat. Imagine the freezer space you'd need!

In urban areas, neighborhood potlucks are built around pots of moose chili or pans of lasagna made with sweet, lean moose meat. Even families that don't have a hunter can usually get meat from a friend. Or, if they're particularly industrious and have tools for butchering, they can wait for a moose to get hit crossing a highway. Hundreds of the animals die that way each year, and the state keeps a list of people waiting their turn to salvage the meat.

In rural areas, where trips to the grocery store are infrequent or impossible, moose meat means survival. Meat is frozen or dried into jerky. Heads are boiled into soup and even the nose is eaten. Boiled until it is soft, it's considered quite a delicacy.

Some Alaska Natives rely on wild food such as moose for as much as half of their diet. Hunters share the choice parts of a moose with elders and others in the village. The animal is so much a part of Native life that cooks at the new, state-of-the-art Alaska Native Hospital in Anchorage simmer up batches of moose soup. For the hospital's patients, a bowl of moose broth is much more healing than chicken soup.

Cured Oven-Roasted Duck Breasts with Dried Cherry and Green Peppercorn Sauce

Mark Linden, Glacial Reflections Catering

This recipe uses a very small amount of curing salt to set the color and texture of the Muscovy duck breast. With this breed of duck, the breast meat is best served medium rare. To cook it any longer toughens the meat and turns it a pale green-gray color. Marinating it is a way to prevent this from happening; the longer it marinates, the better. The curing salt will keep the duck meat moist during the cooking process and give it a nice color. If you don't like medium-rare duck, you can substitute Long Island duck breast and cook it medium well. Keep in mind that the breasts continue to cook after they are removed from the oven.

DUCK BREASTS
1 teaspoon curing salt
½ cup cranberry juice
½ cup apple juice
1 tablespoon pickling spice
2 teaspoons chopped garlic
2 teaspoons chopped shallots
1 teaspoon chopped ginger
2 tablespoons cider vinegar
5 tablespoons olive oil
4 Muscovy duck breasts, trimmed

DRIED CHERRY AND GREEN PEPPERCORN SAUCE
¼ cup sugar
1 teaspoon fresh lemon juice
¼ cup brandy
1 cup Port
1 cinnamon stick
2 star anise
1 cardamom pod
1 teaspoon green peppercorns, mashed
1 bay leaf
½ cup tomato purée

3 cups Beef Stock (page 198) or good-quality canned broth

2 ounces dried cherries

6 tablespoons cherry juice

- To prepare the duck, combine the salt, cranberry and apple juice, pickling spice, garlic, shallots, ginger, and vinegar in a saucepan and heat gently until the salt dissolves. Refrigerate until chilled.

- Add 2 tablespoons of the olive oil and the duck breasts. Marinate, refrigerated, overnight or up to 2 days. Turn halfway through the process.

- Preheat the oven to 350°F.

- Heat a heavy ovenproof skillet or cast-iron skillet on the stove and add the remaining 3 tablespoons of olive oil. Sear the breasts on both sides and finish in the oven for about 10 minutes, or until they reach the doneness you desire. Remove the breasts and allow to rest in a warm place before slicing.

- To make the sauce, combine the sugar and lemon juice in a heavy saucepan and cook over medium heat until it turns golden brown. Carefully add the brandy, Port, cinnamon, star anise, cardamom, green peppercorns, and bay leaf. Simmer 10 minutes. Add the tomato purée, stir well, and reduce by half. Strain, set aside the liquid, and discard the solids.

- Add the stock, dried cherries, and cherry juice. Bring to a steady simmer and reduce by half or until the sauce lightly coats the back of a spoon. Serve hot.

- Spoon the sauce over the duck breasts and serve.

Serves four

Roast Cornish Hen with King Prawn

Al Levinsohn, Alyeska Resort

In Alaska, spot prawns come into season in April and are available fresh until October. This dish takes Alaska's best prawns and mixes them with a game bird. What a terrific surprise to find a tender prawn nestled inside a Cornish hen. Call it an Alaska twist on the old surf and turf.

2 Cornish hens (22 to 24 ounces each)
2 cups Chicken Stock (page 197) or canned chicken broth
4 large (10 count) prawns or 8 smaller Alaska spot prawns
½ cup cilantro, chopped
½ cup purple or sweet basil leaves, chopped
4 cloves garlic, sliced thin
1 tablespoon minced fresh ginger
2 teaspoons low-sodium soy sauce
2 tablespoons olive oil
1 tablespoon fresh lemon juice
Salt and pepper
¾ cup julienned carrot
¾ cup julienned celery
¾ cup julienned onion
2 Japanese eggplant, cut in half lengthwise
1 tablespoon olive oil
1 tablespoon rice vinegar
¼ teaspoon salt
Pinch of black pepper
1 teaspoon *sambal oelek* (Thai chile sauce, available at Asian markets)
1 tablespoon cilantro leaves, minced

- Remove the giblets, rinse the hens well under cool water, and pat dry. Cut the hens in half with a heavy knife or poultry shears. Cut off the wing tips and the tip joint of the legs. Carefully remove all the bones from each half of the hen without piercing the skin and flesh.

- Add the giblets (except the livers), necks, wing tips, and tip joints to the chicken stock. Simmer over medium heat until reduced by one fourth. Strain and reserve.

- Lay the hen halves on the work surface, skin side down. Distribute the cilantro and basil equally over the cavities of the hens.

- Peel the prawns, except for the tail, and devein. From the inside of the hen, run the tail of the prawn through the empty leg socket until the tail shell protrudes from the end. For smaller prawns, use two.

- Mix together the garlic, ginger, soy sauce, olive oil, lemon juice, ½ teaspoon salt, and a pinch of pepper. Equally divide the mixture, spreading it on top of the cilantro-basil layer. Wrap the hen flesh around the prawn to form a package and tie with twine to hold its shape. Wrap the tail of the prawn with foil to protect it during the cooking process.

- Preheat the oven to 350°F.

- Place the hens in a Dutch oven or large, heavy cast-iron skillet so they don't touch. Roast for 20 minutes.

- Meanwhile, toss the carrot, celery, onion, and eggplant in oil and vinegar and season with ¼ teaspoon salt, and a pinch of pepper.

- Remove from the hens from the oven and place the eggplants, skin side up, around them. Sprinkle the vegetables on top of the hens and eggplant. Pour in ½ cup of stock, cover the pan, and return to the oven for 10 minutes more or until the hens and prawns are cooked through.

- Remove the pan from the oven, move the eggplant on top of the hens, and add the *sambal oelek* and stock. The pan should be hot enough for the stock to reduce slightly. Add the cilantro. Remove the foil from the prawn tails.

- Spoon the eggplant, skin side down, on a warm plate. Top with the vegetables. Remove the hens and cut off the string. For each serving, slice the hen on the bias and arrange on top of the vegetables. Drizzle the outer plate area with the pan sauce, garnish with cilantro sprigs, and serve.

Serves four

Smoked Goose Pies

Kirsten Dixon, Riversong Lodge

This is definitely winter fare, although Dixon does the pot pie theme throughout the year. A prepared demi-glace may be cut in half with chicken stock to make a good, all-purpose stock when you can't make your own.

> 4 sheets (5 inches square) frozen puff pastry
> 3 tablespoons fresh thyme leaves
> Coarsely ground sea salt
> 2 large carrots, peeled
> 2 medium Yukon Gold potatoes, scrubbed and quartered
> 2 large yellow onions, peeled and quartered
> Extra virgin olive oil
> Sea salt and ground black pepper
> 1 cup Beef Stock (page 198), made with beef or veal
> 2 smoked goose breasts (see page 232)

- Preheat the oven to 375°F.

- Sprinkle the puff pastry sheets with 2 tablespoons of the thyme and sea salt. Bake in the oven until puffed and browned, about 7 minutes. Separate the top of the puff pastry from the bottom. Discard the bottoms and set the tops aside.

- Cut off the tops and bottoms of the carrots to make them the same size. Cut the carrots in half lengthwise. Coat the carrot halves, potatoes, and onions lightly with olive oil, season with salt and pepper, and sprinkle with 2 tablespoons of the thyme. Place in a roasting pan. Roast until tender, checking after 20 minutes. Remove the vegetables as they are cooked and set aside in a warm place.

- Warm the stock on top of the stove in a saucepan until it steams. Adjust the heat to maintain the steam. Do not simmer.

- Trim the goose breasts of all fat and discard the fat. Thinly slice the breasts against the grain and gently stir into the steaming stock.

- To assemble, warm 4 wide-rimmed bowls. Place ½ carrot, 2 potato quarters, and 2 onion quarters in each. Divide the goose meat, laying it across the vegetables in each of the bowls. Drizzle the stock remaining in the saucepan over the meat and vegetables. Sprinkle with remaining 1 tablespoon of thyme. Top the dish with a puff pastry top and serve.

> Serves four

Hunter's Pot

Kirsten Dixon, Riversong Lodge

Dixon got the inspiration for this dish on a visit to Alain Ducasse's Le Louis XV in Monte Carlo. She was treated to a tour of the kitchen—not one single woman anywhere. The chef had large, twenty-five-pound bags of *fleur de sel*, a sea salt sold only in small precious jars in Alaska. She loves to serve this dish in the winter to buffalo hunters or wayward travelers along the Iditarod Trail. She uses wide-rimmed white pasta bowls so the dish isn't too crowded. You can buy the specialty meats at Alaska Game Sales (see page 232).

> 4 slices sourdough bread, crust trimmed
> 12 ounces Swiss chard
> 4 carrots, peeled and cut into thick matchsticks
> 4 parsnips, peeled and cut into thick matchsticks
> Salt and pepper
> 2 tablespoons grapeseed oil
> 1 pound venison sausage
> 1 pound rabbit tenderloin or loin
> 1 pound reindeer or venison tenderloin
> 1 tablespoon butter
> 8 ounces foie gras, minced and chilled
> 2 cups Rabbit Foie Gras Jus (page 132)

- Preheat the oven to 350°F.

- Toast the bread until crisp and set aside.

- Clean the Swiss chard and separate the leaves from the stems. Mince the stems and cut the leaves into thin strips. Set aside the stems and leaves.

- Season the carrots and parsnips with a sprinkling of salt and pepper. Place in a baking dish with enough water to cover the bottom of the dish. Cover the dish with aluminum foil. Bake until tender, 30 to 40 minutes. Set aside.

- While the vegetables are baking, heat a small sauté pan over medium heat and add 1 tablespoon of the grapeseed oil. Sauté the chard stems and set aside.

- Place the venison sausage in the oven and roast until hot throughout. Don't fry venison sausage or it will become too dry. Set aside in a warm place.

- Rub the rabbit and reindeer tenderloins with salt and pepper. Pan-sear the tenderloins in the remaining tablespoon of grapeseed oil in a medium pan over medium-high heat. Transfer the tenderloins to the oven and finish cooking. Set aside in a warm place.

- Steam the chard leaves, then toss with the butter. Season with salt and pepper. Set aside in a warm place.

- Sear the foie gras quickly on each side in a very hot pan; do this fast or the foie gras will melt. Spoon the foie gras and any drippings equally among the cooked toasts.

- Heat 4 wide-rimmed bowls. Place 1 toast in the center of each bowl. Slice the sausage, rabbit, and deer. Layer the meats on top of the foie gras. Top with the carrots, parsnips, and Swiss chard leaves. Nest the Swiss chard stems on the side of each toast.

- Ladle the rabbit foie gras jus over the top and serve.

Serves four

Rabbit Foie Gras Jus

This luscious liquid is a fine match for Dixon's Hunter's Pot, but it would also be a stellar compliment to any roasted game.

3 tablespoons olive oil
8 ounces (2 sticks) butter
4½ pounds rabbit scraps and trim, any meat cut into ½-inch cubes
3 carrots
1 head garlic, cut in half
1 stalk celery, trimmed and chopped
Salt and freshly ground pepper
1 ounce foie gras, minced

■ Heat the oil in a large stockpot over medium-high heat. Add the butter, allow it to melt, add the rabbit, and stir to coat. Add the carrots, garlic, celery, salt, and pepper. Cook until the rabbit is browned, then remove the meat and vegetables from the pot. Set aside.

■ Add 1 cup of water to the pot and scrape up all of the browned bits remaining on the bottom of the pan. Simmer the water mixture until almost completely evaporated.

■ Return the meat-vegetable mixture to the pot and cover with cold water. Bring the water to a boil, then reduce the heat to maintain a simmer. Simmer for 3 hours.

■ Remove the meat and vegetables and discard. Strain.

Makes 5 cups

King Fredrik's Favorite Danish-Style Hash

Jens Hansen, Jens' Restaurant and Bodega

King Fredrik must have been a pretty bright fellow. This hash is easy to prepare, yet very elegant and delicious. It reflects Hansen's simple but rich style of cooking. Its hearty nature is typical of how many Alaska chefs cook.

½ cup Clarified Butter (page 205)
2 cups peeled and diced baking potatoes
1½ cups diced onion
12 ounces trimmed beef tenderloin, diced small
½ cup demi-glace (available in specialty food shops)
2 tablespoons Worcestershire sauce
Salt and ground black pepper
4 fried eggs
½ cup chopped parsley

- In a large sauté pan over medium-high heat, heat one third of the butter until it is hot. Add the potatoes and cook until tender. Remove and keep warm.

- Add another third of the butter to the sauté pan and heat over medium heat until hot. Add the onions and cook until soft. Remove and keep warm.

- Add the remaining butter to the sauté pan and heat over medium-high heat until very hot. Add the tenderloin pieces and cook to the desired doneness. Drain any residual fat. Return the cooked potatoes and onions to the pan. Add the demi-glace and Worcestershire and toss to combine all the ingredients. Season with salt and pepper to taste.

- Divide the hot meat mixture among 4 warm plates. Top each with a fried egg. Garnish with parsley and serve.

Serves four

Kodiak Nut Brown Ale Lamb Shanks

Mark Linden, Glacial Reflections Catering

This recipe was designed to capture some of the exotic flavors of dried mushrooms in combination with an Alaska-made ale. Alaska has a handful of breweries that are beginning to sell their beers in the Lower 48. By using dried mushroom powder in addition to flour before the braising process, the flavor of the mushroom comes through. The basic recipe can be used with any meat that requires a lengthy braising period-a pot roast, beef stew or possibly some of that game meat you have in the freezer. Just substitute your cut of meat and cook it until fork tender, which will usually be at least two hours.

> 4 lamb shanks
> ½ teaspoon salt
> Pinch of ground black pepper
> ½ tablespoon mesquite seasonings
> 2 tablespoons dried mushroom powder
> ¼ cup flour
> 2 tablespoons cornmeal
> ¼ cup olive oil
> ½ carrot, sliced
> ½ white onion, peeled and sliced
> 1 stalk celery, sliced
> 3 mushrooms, sliced
> ¼ cup brandy
> 12 ounces Kodiak Nut Brown Ale or any good dark beer
> ¾ cup red wine
> 5 juniper berries
> 2 bay leaves
> 1½ teaspoons dried whole-leaf thyme
> ½ cup tomato purée
> 1½ cups Chicken Stock (page 197) or canned chicken broth

- Preheat the oven to 350°F.

- Season the shanks with salt, pepper, and mesquite seasonings.

- Mix together the mushroom powder, flour, and cornmeal, and dredge the shanks in this mixture, coating all sides. Shake off the excess and set aside.

- Heat the oil in a Dutch oven over medium-high heat until it shimmers. Brown the shanks on all sides. Do not allow particles in the pan to burn. Remove the shanks and set aside. Add the carrot, onion, celery, and mushrooms and cook until lightly browned. Add the brandy, ale, wine, juniper berries, bay, thyme, and tomato purée, bring to a low boil, and reduce by half. Add the stock and bring to a boil. Add the shanks, cover, and place in the oven.

- Cook, turning every 30 minutes, until the meat is very tender, 2$\frac{1}{2}$ to 3 hours. Remove the shanks from the pan and keep warm. Skim any excess fat from the liquid in the pan. Cook the liquid slowly until it thickens enough to coat the back of a spoon. Strain.

- Serve the shanks with the sauce, pouring an equal portion over each one.

Serves 4

Braised Lamb Shanks with Sweet-and-Sour Onions

Farrokh Larijani, Glacier BrewHouse

Lamb shanks, long neglected by many cooks in the United States, have come into their own. Braising ensures a tender, succulent result for this cut of lamb. Larijani provides an exciting surprise of flavors with the onion garnish. Polenta is a natural match for this dish.

BRAISING LIQUID

8 cups unsalted Chicken Stock (page 197) or canned chicken broth

1 sprig of rosemary

2 sprigs of thyme

4 cloves roasted garlic

2 cups Beef Stock (page 198) or canned beef broth

LAMB SHANKS

4 lamb shanks (12 ounces each)

1 tablespoon kosher salt

1 teaspoon ground black pepper

2 tablespoons vegetable oil

1 medium onion, chopped

2 stalks celery, chopped

1 cup chopped carrots

2 cups dry red wine

2 cloves garlic

1 bay leaf

½ teaspoon dried thyme leaves

SWEET-AND-SOUR ONIONS

½ cup white balsamic vinegar

3 tablespoons sugar

1 cup yellow pearl onions, blanched and peeled

1 cup red pearl onions, blanched and peeled (see Note)

GARNISH

3 tablespoons olive oil

4 Roma tomatoes, cored, seeded, and diced (½ inch)

½ cup Kalamata olives, pitted and quartered

4 tablespoons thinly sliced basil

1 teaspoon ground black pepper

- To prepare the braising liquid, combine the chicken stock, rosemary, thyme, and garlic in a large saucepan and bring to a boil. Reduce by three fourths. Add the beef stock, strain, and use the liquid to braise shanks.

- Preheat the oven to 350°F.

- To prepare the lamb shanks, season the shanks with salt and pepper. Heat the oil in a heavy-gauge ovenproof pan or Dutch oven until it shimmers. Add the shanks and brown well on all sides. Add the onion, celery, and carrots and continue to brown over moderate heat. Add the red wine and reduce by half. Add the garlic, bay leaf, thyme, and 4 cups of the braising liquid, bring to a simmer, cover, and braise until the shanks are fork tender, about 2½ to 3 hours. Remove the shanks, cover, and set aside in a warm place. Strain the braising liquid and set aside.

- To prepare the sweet-and-sour onions, bring the vinegar to a boil in a large skillet, add the sugar, and cook over medium-high heat until it is dissolved. Add the onions and continue to cook until the onions are well coated and caramelized. Remove from the pan and let cool at room temperature. Set aside.

- To prepare the garnish, heat the olive oil in a skillet until it starts to shimmer. Add the onions, the tomatoes, and the olives. Toss just to heat through. Add 2 cups of the braising liquid and continue to cook until hot. Remove from the heat and add the basil and pepper. Taste to check for seasoning; a bit of salt may be required.

- Place the lamb shanks on 4 warm plates. Spoon the garnish equally over each shank.

- Note: If red pearl onions are unavailable, increase yellow pearl onions to 2 cups.

Serves four

Linguine Carbonara

Kirk McLean, Fiddlehead Restaurant and Bakery

Pasta, whether in Asian or Italian dishes, is as common in Alaska as it is anywhere else on the West Coast. McLean's version of this traditional Italian dish, which uses Italian sausage instead of pancetta, is much like one you might find in any trattoria. The emphasis is on simplicity, both in ingredients and method.

Salt
1 pound bulk Italian sausage
1 medium red bell pepper, seeded and cut into thin strips
12 ounces linguine
2½ ounces prosciutto, sliced very thin and chopped
1 egg
5 ounces Parmigiano-Reggiano, grated
1 cup minced parsley
Salt and freshly ground black pepper

- Put a large pot of salted water on to boil.

- Heat a large sauté pan until hot. Crumble the Italian sausage, add to the hot pan, and brown. Add the peppers and continue to cook for 3 minutes.

- Add the linguine to the boiling water. Return to a boil and cook until just tender. Stir from time to time so that the linguine does not stick together.

- Add the prosciutto to the sausage mixture and remove from the heat.

- Whisk the egg in a large bowl.

- Drain the linguine when cooked; do not rinse. Add to the egg, tossing to coat. Add the Parmigiano and parsley and toss to coat. Add the sausage mixture and toss to combine. Taste and adjust the seasoning with salt and pepper.

- Divide among 4 warm pasta bowls and serve.

Serves four

Migas with Avocado-Tomatillo Sauce

Alev Manalp, Sacks Cafe

Ever since the Russians arrived in the territory in the 1700s, immigrants have influenced food in Alaska. Anchorage has a small but active Latino community and several good cooks whose families come from Mexico. This lovely traditional dish would make a good start to the day or a perfect late-evening meal, served with warm corn tortillas.

AVOCADO-TOMATILLO SAUCE

2 cloves garlic, minced
5 medium tomatillos, peeled and washed
1 jalapeño, chopped (seeded if you like mild sauce)
½ cup chopped cilantro
1 ripe avocado
Salt

MIGAS

1 medium red bell pepper, sliced thin
1 medium red onion, finely diced
2 small jalapeños, finely diced (seeded if you like mild migas)
4 cloves garlic, minced
4 tomatoes, cored and diced small
½ teaspoon salt
2 tablespoons vegetable oil
¾ pound chorizo sausage, crumbled
10 eggs, beaten
½ cup grated sharp cheddar
½ cup grated Monterey Jack
½ cup chopped cilantro
Salt

- To make the avocado-tomatillo sauce, put all the ingredients in a food processor and pulse until chunky.

- To make the migas, combine the red bell pepper, red onion, jalapeños, garlic, tomatoes, and salt. Heat the oil in a large, heavy skillet until it shimmers. Sauté the chorizo until it is browned. Add the vegetable mixture and continue to cook until the onions and peppers just begin to soften. Add the eggs and stir constantly until cooked to desired consistency. Add the cheddar, Monterey Jack, and the cilantro and stir until cheese is melted. Taste and adjust the seasoning with salt.

■ Divide the migas among 4 hot plates and serve with the sauce.

Serves four

Pan-Roasted Chicken Breasts with Chèvre-Herb Stuffing

Farrokh Larijani, Glacier BrewHouse

In a world packed with chicken breast recipes, this recipe stands out. The goat cheese stuffing not only adds flavor, it also contributes moisture to the breast.

FOCACCIA CROUTONS
2 tablespoons butter
4 focaccia, cut into 3-inch circles

CHÈVRE-HERB STUFFING
4 tablespoons butter, salted
3 ounces chèvre
2 cloves garlic, minced
2 tablespoons chopped basil
1 teaspoon minced fresh thyme
½ teaspoon chopped fresh marjoram
½ teaspoon minced rosemary
1 tablespoon thinly sliced green onion
3 tablespoons grated parmesan
Pinch of crushed red pepper
¼ teaspoon coarsely ground black pepper
½ teaspoon granulated onion
½ teaspoon granulated garlic
½ teaspoon kosher salt

CHICKEN BREASTS
4 chicken breasts, skin on (5 ounces each)
1 tablespoon chopped fresh thyme
1 tablespoon chopped rosemary
1 tablespoon chopped sage
1 tablespoon chopped fresh oregano
1 teaspoon crushed red pepper
1 teaspoon kosher salt
4 tablespoons olive oil
3 cups small-diced onion
⅓ cup small-diced roasted red pepper

¾ cup Chicken Stock (page 197) or canned chicken broth
1 tablespoon fresh lemon juice
1 teaspoon black pepper

- To make the croutons, melt the butter and sauté the focaccia over moderate heat until golden brown. Set aside.

- To make the chèvre-herb stuffing, process all the ingredients in a food processor until smooth. Scrape down the sides. Process again until smooth. Refrigerate. Soften slightly for use.

- Preheat the oven to 350°F.

- Trim the fat from the chicken breasts. Insert 1½ tablespoons of the stuffing between the skin and flesh of each chicken breast. Mix together the thyme, rosemary, sage, oregano, red pepper, and salt. Sprinkle 1 tablespoon of the herb mix on top of each breast. Refrigerate.

- Heat the oil in a heavy ovenproof pan until it shimmers. Sear the chicken, skin side down, until golden. Turn the chicken over, place the pan in the oven, and roast until cooked through, 12 to 15 minutes. Check with a paring knife to ensure that there is no pink. Remove the chicken and keep warm.

- Drain the excess oil from the pan and add the onion and pepper. Add the chicken broth and lemon juice and whisk in the remaining stuffing. Season with black pepper, place on medium-high heat, and simmer until the liquid is almost entirely reduced.

- Place the croutons on 4 warm plates and pour the pan sauce equally over all of the croutons, letting the sauce pool onto the plate. Top with the cooked chicken breasts and serve.

Serves four

Pistachio-Crusted Rack of Lamb with Port-Olive Sauce

Elizabeth King, Southside Bistro

In Anchorage, Alaska's biggest city, chefs often impress guests with surprising twists of sophistication. This is one of those dishes. A mustard meringue and the Kalamata olive sauce make it a memorable alternative to the standard rack of lamb. This dish is great with Goat Cheese Mashed Potatoes (page 174).

PORT-OLIVE SAUCE
1 cup ruby Port
1 teaspoon chopped garlic
2 teaspoons chopped shallots
1 sprig of rosemary
Zest of 1 orange
⅔ cup demi-glace (available in specialty food shops)
¼ cup sliced Kalamata olives
Salt and ground black pepper

LAMB
⅓ cup shelled pistachios
½ cup panko (Japanese bread crumbs, available in Asian markets and some supermarkets)
1 tablespoon chopped Italian parsley
¼ teaspoon salt
Pinch of ground black pepper
2 racks of lamb, frenched (7 to 8 bones each)
Salt and ground black pepper
2 tablespoons olive oil
2 egg whites
Pinch of cream of tartar
1 tablespoon Dijon mustard
1 teaspoon fresh thyme leaves

■ Preheat the oven to 400°F.

■ To make the sauce, combine the Port, garlic, shallots, rosemary, and orange zest in a medium saucepan and simmer until the liquid is reduced by a third. Strain and return the liquid to the saucepan. Add the demi-glace, bring to a boil, remove from heat, add olives, and season with salt and pepper.

- Combine the pistachios, panko, salt, and pepper in a food processor. Process until the nuts are chopped very fine.

- Wrap each bone of the lamb in aluminum foil to prevent burning and season the meat lightly with salt and pepper. Pour the olive oil into a very hot skillet, add the lamb, and sear all sides of the chops until browned, about 8 minutes; remove and cool.

- Put the egg whites and cream of tartar in a clean bowl and whip to stiff peaks. Fold in the mustard. Coat the top side of each rack with the mustard meringue. Press the pistachio mixture on top of meringue. Roast the racks to the desired doneness, about 15 minutes for rare. Allow racks to rest 10 minutes before carving. Remove aluminum foil from ribs. As the racks rest, reheat the sauce to a simmer. Add the fresh thyme. Carve racks into chops; pool sauce around and over, and serve.

Serves four

Brined Rosemary Roasted Chicken

Kirk McLean, Fiddlehead Restaurant and Bakery

This is a dish that warms the whole house and allows you to use a great technique: brining. Brining before roasting makes a chicken succulent and flavorful. It does tend to be saltier, so take care in adding any additional salt before roasting and use pan drippings sparingly if you make pan gravy. Serve this with soft polenta or mashed potatoes.

> 1 gallon cold water
> 2 cups kosher salt
> 2 cups honey
> 1 broiler chicken (about 2 pounds)
> ¼ cup olive oil
> Cracked black pepper
> 6 sprigs of rosemary, roughly chopped
> 10 cloves garlic

■ Mix the water, kosher salt, and honey in a large container able to fit in your refrigerator until the salt dissolves. This is the brine.

■ Remove the giblets from inside the chicken. Set aside for another use.

■ Rinse the chicken well under cold running water. Completely immerse the chicken in the brine and refrigerate for 24 hours. If a portion of the chicken floats above the brine, place a plate or bowl on top of the chicken and add some weight to the plate or bowl to keep the chicken submerged.

■ When ready to cook, preheat the oven to 350°F.

■ Remove the chicken from the brine and discard the brine. Rinse the chicken well and pat dry with paper towels. Brush or rub all of the chicken skin with olive oil and season with pepper. Insert the rosemary and the garlic cloves into the cavity of the chicken.

■ Place the chicken on a rack in a roasting pan and roast until an instant-read thermometer indicates 165°F to 170°F when inserted in the thigh without touching the bone, about 1½ hours.

■ Tent the chicken with aluminum foil and let rest in a warm place for 15 minutes before carving. Chef McLean likes to serve it with soft polenta or mashed potatoes.

Serves four

Rosemary-Cured Lamb Rack with Savory Mustard Crust

Kirk McLean, Fiddlehead Restaurant and Bakery

The curing of the lamb gives the meat a particularly succulent character.

1 quart boiling water
1 cup honey
1 cup kosher salt
1 cup rosemary leaves
1 tablespoon black pepper
¼ cup cider vinegar
2 full lamb racks, frenched
¼ cup Dijon mustard
½ cup panko (Japanese bread crumbs, available in Asian markets and some supermarkets)
1 tablespoon fresh thyme leaves
2 tablespoons grated parmesan
2 tablespoons minced garlic

- In a large saucepan combine the water, honey, salt, rosemary, black pepper, and vinegar to make the cure. Boil for 3 minutes. Cool in an ice-water bath.

- Immerse the lamb racks in the cold cure. Refrigerate for 3 to 4 hours.

- Preheat the oven to 400°F.

- For the crust, mix the mustard, panko, thyme, parmesan, and garlic in a bowl. Remove the racks from the cure, rinse, and pat dry. Wrap each individual bone in aluminum foil so that the bones will not burn in the oven. Divide the crust mixture in two and spread on the meat side of the racks. Place the racks in a roasting pan, crust side up. Roast to the desired doneness, about 15 minutes for rare. Allow racks to rest 10 minutes before carving.

- Remove the foil from the bones and cut each rack equally in half. Serve each portion on a warm plate.

Serves four

Grilled Skirt Steak with Tequila Vinaigrette

Farrokh Larijani, Glacier BrewHouse

Cool salad greens with untraditional garnishes, a unique dressing, and hot, flavorful steak fresh off of the grill topped with a great puréed salsa—this is a main course salad that seems at first glance to be very involved. In fact, the dish is quite simple and refreshing on a sunny barbecue day. It was inspired by Mike Jones, one of Larijani's cooks, who invented the salsa. Look for the smoked paprika at a Mexican grocery or Tex-Mex store.

MEAT RUB
2½ teaspoons kosher salt
½ teaspoon ground black pepper
½ medium yellow onion, thinly sliced
2 tablespoons chopped cilantro
Juice of 1 lime
1 cup brown ale
2 tablespoons paprika (preferably smoked)
1 teaspoon puréed kiwi
1¾ pounds skirt steak or flank steak

TEQUILA VINAIGRETTE
2 tablespoons minced shallots
½ cup bottled margarita mix
½ teaspoon minced lime zest
½ tablespoon fresh lime juice
2 tablespoons tequila
1¼ teaspoons kosher salt
¼ teaspoon ground black pepper
1 tablespoon chopped cilantro
½ cup vegetable oil

SALSA
3 medium tomatoes, cored, seeded, and chopped
4 cups water
¼ cup diced red bell pepper
¼ cup diced green bell pepper

4 jalapeños (seeded if you like mild salsa)

½ medium yellow onion, chopped

2 cloves garlic, chopped

½ teaspoon ground cumin

1½ teaspoons kosher salt

½ cup chopped cilantro

2 teaspoons fresh oregano leaves, minced

SALAD

4 cups salad greens

4 cups mesclun mix

¾ cup papaya and mango chunks

1¼ cups seeded Roma tomatoes, cut in large dice

½ cup thinly sliced red onion

8 baby corn (optional)

1 cup snow peas, cut into thin strips (optional)

- To make the meat rub, mix the kosher salt, black pepper, onion, cilantro, lime juice, ale, paprika, and kiwi to make a thin paste.

- Trim the steak of any fat. Rub the seasoning mixture onto all surfaces of the meat, cover, and refrigerate for 10 hours. Turn the meat over after 5 hours.

- To make the tequila vinaigrette, combine shallots, margarita mix, lime zest, lime juice, tequila, salt, pepper, and cilantro in a medium bowl and mix. Whisk in the oil in a thin, steady stream. Set aside.

- To make the salsa, place the tomatoes, water, bell peppers, jalapeños, onion, garlic, cumin, and salt in a large saucepan, bring to a boil, and cook until the water is reduced by two thirds. Purée the reduced mixture in a food processor. Stir in the cilantro and oregano. Check the seasoning for salt. Set aside.

- Preheat the grill.

- Remove the meat from the refrigerator. Grill the meat over hot coals until cooked to the desired doneness. Remove the meat from the grill, tent with foil, and set aside in a warm place for 10 minutes before carving.

- Meanwhile, make the salad. Combine the salad greens, mesclun mix, papaya and mango, tomatoes, onion, and corn and snow peas, if using. Toss with 1 cup of the vinaigrette, setting aside the remaining vinaigrette for another day. Divide the dressed salad among 4 plates.

- Slice the beef into thin strips at an angle across the grain of the meat. Arrange the meat around the salads. Spoon the salsa on top of the meat and serve.

Serves four

Stuffed Pork Chops with Oven-Roasted Herbed Tomatoes

Farrokh Larijani, Glacier BrewHouse

Polenta would be a great addition to these chops.

CURING BRINE
3 teaspoons crushed garlic cloves
4 cups water
3 tablespoons kosher salt
1 tablespoon sugar
½ teaspoon dried thyme
1 tablespoon black peppercorns
½ bay leaf
Pinch of mustard seeds
Pinch of crushed red pepper
Pinch of crushed star anise

PORK CHOPS
4 bone-in pork chops (12 ounces each)
8 ounces sweet Sicilian sausage or bulk Italian sausage, cooked
¼ cup thinly sliced basil
¼ cup brandy
1 ¼ cups Beef Stock (page 198) or high-quality canned beef broth
2 cups Oven-Roasted Herbed Tomatoes (page 175)
3 tablespoons pine nuts, toasted
4 sprigs of sage

■ To make the curing brine, place all the ingredients into a pot and bring to a boil. Simmer for 10 minutes. Cool. Refrigerate.

■ Place the pork chops in the cold brine and refrigerate for 24 hours.

■ Preheat the grill. Preheat the oven to 450°F.

- Remove the chops from the brine. Drain. With a boning knife or paring knife, cut a pocket into each chop. Stuff each chop with the cooked sausage and basil. Grill the chops for 3 minutes on each side, then place in a sauté pan just large enough to hold them. Roast in the oven until an instant-read thermometer registers 155°F. Remove the chops from the pan, tent with aluminum foil, and keep warm.

- Place the sauté pan over medium-high heat and add brandy. Scrape the pan with a wooden spoon to release drippings. Add the stock, bring to a boil, and reduce the mixture to a syrupy consistency.

- Place the chops on 4 warm plates and drizzle the pan sauce over the pork. Garnish with the tomatoes, pine nuts, and a sage sprig.

Serves four

Tamales

Sean Maryott, The Homestead

Good tamales are hard to find in Alaska. There are plenty of Mexican restaurants, but many only take the time to make this classic dish for holidays or other special occasions. This recipe makes fluffy, sophisticated tamales.

> 8 ounces cooked and shredded pork shoulder
>
> 2 roasted red jalapeños, peeled and minced
>
> 1 jumbo yellow onion, sliced, grilled, and minced
>
> ½ cup minced cilantro
>
> 2½ teaspoons sea salt
>
> ¼ cup tequila
>
> 1 package dried corn husks (available at Mexican grocery stores and some supermarkets)
>
> 2 cups masa harina
>
> 1⅓ cups Chicken Stock (page 197), warm
>
> ½ cup pork lard
>
> ¼ cup whipping cream
>
> 2 teaspoons baking powder
>
> 3 tablespoons goat cheese

- For the filling, combine pork, jalapeños, onion, cilantro, ½ teaspoon of the salt, and tequila in a bowl. Refrigerate the pork filling.

- Soak the dried corn husks in warm water until pliable, drain, and set aside.

- While the husks are soaking, make the masa dough. Mix the masa harina and stock together in a bowl that will fit on a mixer. Let the mixture rest 20 minutes. Place the bowl on a mixer, add the lard, and beat on high speed until the mixture is fluffy and smooth. Mix the cream, the remaining 2 teaspoons of sea salt, and the baking powder in a cup. With the mixer on slow, add the cream mixture to the masa mixture. Set aside.

- Lay the husks out on a flat surface. Trim them to about 8 x 4 inches. Beginning at the bottom edge of the husks, spread ¼ cup of the masa mixture (4 x 3 inches), using a rubber spatula. Place 1 heaping tablespoon of the pork filling on top of the masa. Add 1 rounded teaspoon of goat cheese on top of that. Wrap the husks around the filling lengthwise, then fold over and tie with a thin strip of leftover husk. Proceed until all the tamales are finished.

- Fill a steamer pan until the water comes to within 1 inch of the bottom of the steamer insert. Bring the water to a simmer. Fill the steamer insert with the tamales. Place the insert over the simmering water and cover. Steam for 30 minutes. Turn off the heat and let the tamales rest for 30 minutes more, or until the masa is cooked through and the filling is hot.

- Place tamales on 4 warm plates. They are great served with Chili Verde (page 123) and a cold beer.

    Serves four

Pan-Seared Venison Medallions with Raspberry—Green Peppercorn Sauce

Elizabeth King, Southside Bistro

At the restaurant, they use farm-raised venison from New Zealand, but you can substitute your own game deer. Caribou or elk would also work well, as would veal. As an accompaniment, try Sweet Onion Jam (page 195) and Twice-Baked Gorgonzola Potatoes (page 173).

1½ pounds venison loin medallions
Kosher salt and ground black pepper
1 tablespoon chopped fresh thyme
½ cup fresh or frozen unsweetened raspberries
1½ tablespoons dried green peppercorns
¾ cup ruby Port
3 tablespoons chopped shallots
¾ cup demi-glace (available in specialty food shops)
2 tablespoons olive oil
4 tablespoons butter, chilled, cut into 4 equal pieces

- Space out the medallions on a cutting board and cover with plastic wrap. Gently pound the medallions with a mallet or heavy pan so that they are equal in thickness (about ½ inch) and shape. Season with salt and pepper and sprinkle with 1 teaspoon of the thyme. Refrigerate until ready to cook.

- Combine the raspberries, peppercorns, Port, and shallots in a medium saucepan. Reduce this mixture by half over high heat. Add the demi-glace and the remainder of the thyme. Simmer on lowest heat while you cook the venison.

- Heat the oil in a large skillet until it shimmers. Add the medallions and brown very well on each side. Medium-rare is best. Remove from the pan and keep warm.

- Return the sauce to a rolling boil and remove from the heat. Whip in the butter pieces one by one, allowing each piece to melt before adding another. Taste the sauce and adjust with salt and pepper.

- Divide the medallions among 4 warm plates, spoon on the sauce, and serve.

Serves four

Zinfandel-Braised Lamb Shanks

Kirk McLean, Fiddlehead Restaurant and Bakery

Good wine is the key to this dish. Never cook with any wine you wouldn't pour in a glass and drink. The wine doesn't have to be expensive, but it has to taste good. Polenta, potatoes, or cannellini beans go well with this dish.

4 lamb shanks (12 ounces each)
1 tablespoon salt
1 teaspoon ground black pepper
2 tablespoons olive oil
2 medium yellow onions, diced
8 cloves garlic, peeled
750 ml California zinfandel, good quality
4 cups unsalted Chicken Stock (page 197) or canned chicken broth
3 sprigs of rosemary

- Preheat the oven to 350°F.

- Season shanks with salt and pepper. Heat the oil in a cast-iron or heavy ovenproof skillet or Dutch oven until it shimmers. Brown the shanks on all sides, remove, and set aside. Add the onions and garlic to the skillet and cook, stirring until the onions are translucent.

- Add 2 cups of the wine and bring to a boil. Add the remainder of the wine, chicken stock, and the rosemary and bring to a boil. Add the shanks, cover, and transfer to the oven. Braise the shanks until very tender, 2½ to 3 hours. Remove the shanks from the pan and keep warm.

- Strain the remaining liquid from the pan. Set aside the liquid and purée the solids in a blender or food processor. Add to the liquid and reduce over medium-high heat until the sauce begins to thicken. Add the shanks and heat until hot throughout.

- Serve the shanks with the sauce divided equally over each.

Serves four

Garden Love

Sean Maryott, The Homestead

This vegan dish is very well rounded nutritionally and has complex flavors. In Alaska, cooks have to look hard for items like fresh broccoli rabe and fresh fava beans— especially in winter. That makes this dish a real treat up north. In this dish, Maryott likes to add six to nine sautéed fresh anchovies (headed and gutted, of course) to the fava beans while they are simmering. Then it's not vegan anymore, but, he says, "the slight backbones give definition to the dish."

6 spring onions (3 inches in diameter), chopped
3 tablespoons olive oil
2 cups fresh fava beans
8 ounces fresh broccoli rabe
8 ounces fresh mustard greens
8 ounces fresh collard greens
8 ounces arugula
8 ounces Swiss chard
8 ounces baby bok choy
3 Thai red chiles, seeds removed, chopped
Sea salt
3 cups steamed organic brown rice

■ Sauté the green onions in 1 tablespoon of the olive oil until lightly browned. Set aside. Poach the fava beans in 2 cups boiling water until tender. Shuck. Set aside. Wash all of the greens thoroughly. Remove the leaves from the stems. Set aside the leaves.

■ Heat the remaining 2 tablespoons olive oil in a large wok over high heat until it shimmers. Add the chiles, stir, and sear the greens in batches. Add 1 or 2 tablespoons of water to ensure that the leaves do not burn. Combine all of the greens with the reserved onions and fava beans and season with salt.

■ Mix the vegetables with the rice and serve.

Serves four

Grilled Fusion Tofu

Sean Maryott, The Homestead

You might shake your head when you read the ingredient list, but you'll find the recipe is worth the effort. If you have to cut out any steps, probably skipping the grill would be the one. If you cut out the Thai fish sauce, this is a lacto-vegetarian dish of the gods.

TOFU MARINADE

2 teaspoons minced ginger

2 teaspoons minced garlic

¼ cup tamarind concentrate (available in Asian markets)

¼ cup frozen orange juice concentrate

1 tablespoon Thai fish sauce (available in Asian markets), optional

2 tablespoons soy sauce

2 teaspoons toasted sesame oil

¼ cup honey

¼ cup (packed) chopped cilantro

TOFU

12 ounces firm tofu

1 tablespoon vegetable oil

12 ounces pasta, such as conchiglie or fusilli

2 tablespoons olive oil

¾ cup chopped red onion

1 tablespoon minced garlic

¾ cup diced Roma tomatoes

⅓ cup chopped Kalamata olives

⅓ cup white wine

1 tablespoon chopped parsley

1 tablespoon butter

¼ cup crumbled feta cheese

¼ cup thinly sliced green onion

2 cups fresh greens, such as Swiss chard or spinach,
    roughly chopped and blanched

1 teaspoon coriander seeds, toasted and crushed

¼ teaspoon grated nutmeg

Sea salt and ground white pepper

4 tablespoons grated aged provolone or parmesan or Romano

- Preheat the grill.

- To make the marinade, place the ginger, garlic, tamarind, orange juice concentrate, fish sauce, soy sauce, sesame oil, honey, and cilantro in a food processor and process until smooth. Set aside.

- Gently squeeze the excess moisture from the tofu and cut it into 4 equal pieces. Brush 1 side of the tofu with the vegetable oil. Place the oiled side of the tofu on the hot grill and cook for 3 minutes. Transfer the grilled tofu in the marinade and marinate for 1 hour.

- Preheat the oven to 350°F.

- Put 4 quarts of salted water on to boil for the pasta.

- Roast the tofu in the oven for 30 minutes. Slice and keep warm.

- Cook the pasta until just tender and drain.

- While the tofu is in the oven and the pasta is cooking, heat the olive oil in a heavy skillet over medium-high heat until the oil shimmers. Add the red onion and cook until it begins to soften. Add the garlic, stir, then immediately add the tomatoes, olives, wine, parsley, and butter. When the butter is melted, add the feta, green onions, fresh greens, coriander, and nutmeg. Taste and adjust the seasoning with salt and pepper.

- Divide pasta among 4 large bowls. Top with the tomato mixture, then with the tofu slices. Garnish with provolone and serve.

Serves four

Marinated Fresh Tomato and Basil Pasta with Gorgonzola and Chèvre

JoAnn Asher, Sacks Cafe

This dish lends itself to variations with many additional ingredients, such as Alaska spot shrimp or other shrimp (about ¾ pound), lightly sautéed with crushed red pepper and a pinch of salt, or coarsely chopped green and Kalamata olives (½ cup each).

4 large vine-ripened tomatoes, cored and chopped
¼ cup minced garlic
1 tablespoon capers, drained
3 tablespoons balsamic vinegar
¼ cup extra virgin olive oil
Salt and ground black pepper
1 pound pasta, such as linguine or penne
1 cup crumbled Gorgonzola
3 ounces chèvre or other soft goat cheese
½ cup chopped basil

- Bring 4 quarts of salted water to a boil.

- Combine the tomatoes, garlic, capers, vinegar, oil, ¾ teaspoon salt, and ¼ teaspoon pepper in a large bowl. Let rest for at least 15 minutes. Just before the pasta is finished cooking, heat the tomato mixture in a large saucepan until hot.

- Cook the pasta until just tender. Drain. Add the pasta to the tomato mixture. Stir in the Gorgonzola and chèvre.

- Divide among 4 large, hot soup bowls. Sprinkle with basil and serve.

Serves four

Grilled Vegetable Napoleons with Rosemary-Corn Relish

Jens Nannestad, Southside Bistro

Increasingly, Alaska restaurant patrons are turning to vegetarian entrées. A vegetarian dish is a must at most good restaurants in Anchorage, and can be found in cities like Juneau and Fairbanks. This dish is proof that vegetarian cuisine need not be boring.

1 head of garlic, peeled and minced
½ cup olive oil
¼ cup balsamic vinegar
Kosher salt and freshly ground black pepper
1 eggplant, sliced ¼ inch thick
1 medium zucchini, sliced ¼ inch thick
1 large yellow squash, sliced ¼ inch thick
1 baking potato, sliced ¼ inch thick
2 ripe tomatoes, sliced ¼ inch thick
Vegetable oil
8 ounces Fontina, mozzarella, or Asiago, grated

ROSEMARY-CORN RELISH
2 ears of corn, husked and silk removed
2 Roma tomatoes, cored
1 sprig of rosemary
2 shallots, peeled and minced
1 teaspoon chipotle pepper paste
2 teaspoons rice wine vinegar

- Preheat the grill.

- Whisk together olive oil, balsamic vinegar, 1 teaspoon salt, and ¼ teaspoon pepper. In separate bowls, marinate the eggplant, zucchini, yellow squash, potato, and tomatoes in the olive oil mixture. Grill the vegetables until tender, remove from the grill, and set aside to cool.

- Preheat the oven to 375°F.

- Lightly oil a baking tray. Assemble 4 napoleons, alternating the different grilled vegetables in stacks with a sprinkle of cheese between each layer. Bake the napoleons until heated through, about 10 minutes.

- To make the relish, cut the kernels off the cobs and blanch in simmering water for 1 minute, remove, and cool. Dice the Roma tomatoes the size of the corn kernels. Mince the rosemary; you should have about 2 tablespoons. Combine the corn, tomatoes, rosemary, and shallots in a bowl. Add the chipotle paste and rice wine vinegar and season to taste with salt and pepper.

- Place the napoleons on warm plates, garnish with relish, and serve.

Serves four

Side Dishes
and Beverages

Wild Mushroom and Potato Hash

Mark Linden, Glacial Reflections Catering

Several species of edible wild mushrooms grow everywhere, from the trails around Sitka to the parks in Anchorage to the hills of Fairbanks. When the snow melts, much of the state is a forager's dream. This recipe is a nice way to showcase mushrooms in a substantial side dish. It can also serve as a light supper paired with a salad, or as a hearty addition to the breakfast table.

> 4 slices thin bacon, minced
> ¼ cup minced onion
> 1 cup wild mushrooms, sliced
> 1 teaspoon minced fresh thyme
> 2 teaspoons minced parsley
> 1 tablespoon thinly sliced chives
> 1 pound baking potatoes, peeled and grated
> ¼ cup cream
> ¼ teaspoon salt
> ¼ teaspoon ground black pepper
> 2 tablespoons butter

■ Preheat the oven to 350°F.

■ Cook the bacon in a sauté pan until brown, remove, and set aside. Cook the onion and mushrooms in the bacon fat over low heat until soft, about 10 minutes. Drain. Add the cooked onions and mushrooms to the reserved bacon, discarding any fat left over in the pan.

■ Add the thyme, parsley, chives, potatoes, cream, salt, and pepper and form into 4 patties. Heat 1 tablespoon of the butter in a sauté pan over medium heat. Add the patties and cook until browned on 1 side. Add the remaining 1 tablespoon butter and brown the other side. Transfer the patties to a baking tray and finish in the oven for 15 minutes, or until cooked through.

■ Serve hot.

> Serves four

Sorbets

Mark Linden, Glacial Reflections Catering

Traditionally, sorbets are enjoyed as a palate cleanser between courses or as a dessert. These sorbets are made with vegetables as the main flavoring. They were devised so that they would go well with salads. Linden was told that the only way the governor of Alaska would eat carrots was in the chef's candied carrot sorbet! In addition to the three flavoring ingredients listed here—beet, cucumber, and onion—you can invent your own.

If you find that you do not have the time to make the syrup used as a base, there are some ready-made lemon sorbets located in the freezer section of your grocery store. Allow the lemon sorbet to soften and whisk in the prepared flavoring agent, chilled. Put your sorbet in the freezer and let it become firm.

Roasted Beet Sorbet

> 1 medium-size beet
> 1 tablespoon vegetable oil
> 1½ tablespoons citrus vodka
> 1½ teaspoons minced fresh ginger
> 1⅛ tablespoons pickling spice
> 1 cup cranberry juice
> 1 cup Basic Syrup, chilled (page 168)

- Preheat the oven to 350°F.

- Cut the ends off the beet, rub the beet with oil, and roast until soft, 2 to 2½ hours. Chill, peel, and chop.

- Combine the vodka, ginger, pickling spice, and cranberry juice in a saucepan, bring to a simmer, and cook 20 minutes. Add the beets and purée in a blender or food processor. Strain, pressing down on the solids to extract all the flavor. Set aside the liquid and discard the solids.

- Blend the liquid with the syrup and freeze in a sorbet machine or ice cream maker. Hold in the freezer until ready to serve.

> Makes about 3 cups

Cucumber Sorbet

> ½ large cucumber, peeled, seeded, and chopped
> 1½ tablespoons rice vinegar
> 1½ tablespoons minced fresh dill
> 1 tablespoon crème de menthe
> 1 cup Basic Syrup, chilled (page 168)

- Purée all the ingredients in a blender or food processor. Strain, pressing down on the solids to extract all the flavor. Set aside the liquid and discard the solids.

- Blend the liquid with the syrup, and freeze in a sorbet machine or ice cream maker. Hold in the freezer until ready to serve.

> Makes 3 cups

Candied Onion Sorbet

> ONION MARMALADE
> 2 tablespoons sugar
> ½ teaspoon water
> 1 red onion
> 1 teaspoon pickling spice
> 2 tablespoons cider vinegar
> 2 tablespoons currant jelly
> Juice of ¼ orange

> SORBET
> 1 cup fresh lemon juice
> 1 cup water
> 1 cup Basic Syrup, chilled (page 168)
> 1 egg white
> 1 cup Onion Marmalade (recipe above)

- To make the onion marmalade, place the sugar in a small saucepan, add the water, and heat over medium heat, without stirring, until lightly caramelized. Add the onion immediately, stir, and cook for 5 minutes. Add the pickling spice, vinegar, currant jelly, and orange juice. Simmer until reduced to a syrup and the onions are cooked through. Purée all the ingredients in a blender or food processor. Set aside 1 cup for the sorbet and use the remainder on a salad.

- To make the sorbet, place the lemon juice, water, and syrup in an ice cream freezer and begin the freezing process. Once the mix has begun to thicken, remove 1 cup of the mix and place it in a bowl. Add the egg white and whip until thick and foamy.

- Return this mix to the ice cream freezer and add the onion marmalade. Finish the freezing process and hold in the freezer until ready to serve.

Makes 3 to 3½ cups

Basic Syrup

⅔ cup sugar
½ cup water

- Combine the sugar and water in a saucepan and bring to a full boil. Remove from the heat and chill thoroughly.

Makes about 1 cup

Saffron Risotto Cakes

Elizabeth King, Southside Bistro

These hearty golden cakes are a nice alternative to steamed rice or potatoes.

> 2 teaspoons olive oil
> ½ small white onion, finely chopped
> 1 teaspoon minced garlic
> 1 cup Arborio rice
> Pinch of saffron
> ½ cup white wine
> 2 cups Vegetable Stock (page 199), Chicken Stock (page 197), or canned chicken broth
> ½ cup grated parmesan
> 2 teaspoons butter
> Salt and ground white pepper
> 1 tablespoon chopped basil
> Semolina flour for dusting
> Olive oil, for frying

- Combine the olive oil, onion, and garlic in a large saucepan. Sauté 1 minute. Add the rice and saffron and stir to coat with oil. Add the wine and reduce by half, stirring constantly.

- Adjust the heat to medium, add one third of the stock, and stir constantly until the stock is almost absorbed by the rice. Add another a third of the stock and stir constantly until it is absorbed. Add the remaining stock and cook until the rice is creamy and just tender. Stir in the parmesan and butter and adjust the seasoning with salt and pepper to taste. Stir in the basil. Spread the risotto in a shallow pan and refrigerate until it can be formed into cakes.

- Form the risotto into 8 cakes, dust with semolina, and pan-fry in the olive oil for 2 minutes on each side, or until golden brown. Serve 2 cakes per person.

Serves four

Polenta Fritters

Jens Nannestad, Southside Bistro

These fried polenta cakes are fun because they can be cut into any shape before frying or grilling. They make a sturdy base for grilled fish or stews or work nicely as a side dish for sweet game meat like caribou or moose.

> 1 cup water or stock
> 1½ teaspoons extra virgin olive oil
> ½ teaspoon salt
> Pinch of ground black pepper
> 1 cup polenta or coarse yellow cornmeal (not instant)
> 1 tablespoon chopped herbs, such as basil, parsley, and oregano

■ Combine the water, oil, salt, and pepper in a medium saucepan and bring to a simmer. Pour in the polenta in a steady, thin stream, stirring constantly. Bring to a simmer, then adjust the heat to low. Cook for 30 minutes, stirring occasionally. Add the herbs and stir to blend.

■ Pour the polenta onto a lightly greased jelly-roll pan to a thickness of ½ inch. Chill for 2 hours.

■ Cut the polenta into desired shapes and grill or sauté until crisp.

Serves four

Soft Polenta

Glenn Denkler

Fresh minced herbs of your choice may be stirred in just before serving.

1 cup water
2 cups milk
1 teaspoon salt
1 cup polenta or coarse yellow cornmeal (not instant)
2 tablespoons butter
¼ cup Parmigiano-Reggiano or high-quality Romano
Salt and ground black pepper

■ Heat the water, milk, and salt to a simmer in a medium-size, heavy-gauge saucepan. Add the polenta in a thin, steady stream, whisking constantly. Bring back to a simmer. Cook for 10 minutes, then taste to determine if the polenta is tender. It may take a little longer using cornmeal. Stir in the butter and cheese. Taste and adjust the seasoning with salt and pepper to taste.

■ Serve immediately.

Serves four

Polenta Croutons

Farrokh Larijani, Orso

These rich, herb-filled croutons can liven soups or round out a salad supper.

1 cup water
½ cup water
¼ teaspoon salt
¾ teaspoon extra virgin olive oil
½ cup polenta
Pinch of ground white pepper
4 tablespoons grated parmesan
¼ teaspoon minced rosemary
¼ teaspoon minced fresh thyme
½ teaspoon minced basil
1 tablespoon heavy cream
2 tablespoons olive oil
Salt and ground black pepper

■ Bring the water, salt, and oil to a boil in a medium saucepan. Add the polenta in a steady stream, whisking constantly. Bring to a simmer. Turn off the heat and let sit, covered, for 1 minute. Add the pepper, 2 tablespoons of the parmesan, the rosemary, thyme, basil, and cream. Stir to blend well.

■ Pour the polenta into a lightly greased square cake pan to a thickness of ½ inch. Press with a spatula so that there are no air bubbles and the polenta is smooth on top. Refrigerate for 3 hours.

■ Cut the polenta into 4 squares and cut again diagonally to form triangles.

■ Heat the olive oil in a sauté pan over medium-high heat until it shimmers. Pan-fry the triangles until golden on each side. Remove from the pan, season with salt and pepper, and sprinkle with the remaining 2 tablespoons of parmesan cheese.

■ Serve hot.

Serves four

Twice-Baked Gorgonzola Potatoes

Elizabeth King, Southside Bistro

An elegant twist on traditional stuffed baked potatoes.

> 16 small red potatoes
> Olive oil
> Salt and ground black pepper
> ⅓ cup crumbled Gorgonzola
> ¼ cup sour cream
> 1 tablespoon thinly sliced chives
> 1 tablespoon butter

- Preheat the oven to 375°F.

- Scrub the potatoes to remove any dirt. Cut off a small piece of each potato so that the potatoes will stand upright. Rub each potato with a small amount of olive oil and season lightly with salt and pepper. Roast the potatoes until tender, about 30 minutes.

- When the potatoes are just cool enough to handle, cut the top quarter off each one. Using a small spoon, scoop out almost all of the potato pulp, leaving a small layer so that the potato can support itself. Place the potato pulp in a bowl and add the Gorgonzola, sour cream, chives, and butter. Mash by hand or with a mixer.

- Preheat the broiler.

- Stuff the filling into each potato and stand the potatoes up on a baking tray. Place under the broiler until the tops are lightly browned.

- Serve hot.

> Serves four

Goat Cheese Mashed Potatoes

Elizabeth King, Southside Bistro

A perfect side for any meat dish and a surprisingly good dish with robust fish dishes.

> 1 pound Yukon Gold potatoes, peeled and chopped
> 2 ounces chèvre or other soft goat cheese
> ¼ cup heavy cream
> 1 tablespoon butter
> Salt and ground black pepper

■ Boil the potatoes in salted water until tender. Drain. Add the chèvre, cream, and butter. Whip or mash by hand. Taste and adjust the seasoning with salt and pepper.

■ Serve hot.

Serves four

Oven-Roasted Herbed Tomatoes

Farrokh Larijani, Glacier BrewHouse

These tomatoes work well as a garnish to grilled meats. Larijani serves them with his Stuffed Pork Chops (page 150).

> 3 cups halved cherry tomatoes
> ¼ cup olive oil
> 1 cup Vegetable Stock (page 199)
> ½ teaspoon crushed red pepper
> ¼ cup grilled leeks
> 3 tablespoons chopped basil
> Salt and ground black pepper

- Preheat the oven to 350°F.

- Mix the tomatoes and olive oil in a small roasting pan. Place in the oven, reduce the temperature to 150°F and roast for 8 hours, or until almost all of the moisture has evaporated from the tomatoes.

- In a small saucepan, heat the stock and red pepper to a boil, then reduce to a simmer. Reduce by three fourths. Add the roasted tomatoes, leeks, and basil. Season with salt and pepper.

- Serve hot. Leftovers may be refrigerated for up to 1 week or frozen for up to 2 months.

> Serves four to six

Fiddlehead and Wild Mushroom Relish

Elizabeth King, Southside Bistro

Spring signals the opening of halibut season, and fiddleheads, the early sprouts of wild ferns, pop up all over. King likes to use Alaskan wild mushrooms when they're available, but varieties such as shiitake or oyster mushrooms would be wonderful in this recipe. If fiddleheads are not available, substitute fresh asparagus tips.

2 tablespoons butter
8 ounces fiddlehead ferns, cleaned and blanched
5 ounces wild mushrooms, sliced
2 teaspoons chopped shallots
2 teaspoons chopped garlic
Salt and pepper
¼ cup dry white wine
2 Roma tomatoes, cored and finely diced
1 tablespoon chopped chives
1 tablespoon chopped basil

■ Heat the butter in a large frying pan over medium-high heat until it sizzles. Add the fiddleheads, mushrooms, shallots, and garlic. Season with salt and pepper, then cook until tender. Add the wine, tomatoes, chives, and basil. Toss until the tomatoes are heated through. Taste and adjust seasoning.

■ Serve hot or refrigerate for up to 3 days.

Serves four

Dill Mustard Potato Salad

Margie Brown, Sacks Cafe

Rarely does a sandwich leave the Sacks kitchen without a side of this well-crafted potato salad.

¼ cup sour cream
½ cup mayonnaise
1 tablespoon Dijon mustard
2 teaspoons chopped fresh dill
1 teaspoon red wine vinegar
2 teaspoons fresh lemon juice
¾ teaspoon salt
¾ teaspoon sugar
½ teaspoon minced garlic
Pinch of celery seeds
½ teaspoon Worcestershire sauce
¼ teaspoon ground black pepper
1 pound red potatoes, scrubbed
1 stalk celery, finely diced
3 tablespoons finely diced red onion

- Mix the sour cream, mayonnaise, mustard, dill, vinegar, lemon juice, salt, sugar, garlic, celery seed, Worcestershire, and pepper in a large bowl. Simmer the potatoes in salted water until fork tender. Peel and slice. Add to the sour cream mixture. Fold in the celery and onion. Adjust the seasoning with salt and pepper.

- Serve cold or refrigerate for up to 5 days.

Serves four

Apple, Cranberry, and Beet Relish

Mark Linden, Glacial Reflections Catering

This is very easy to make and is a wonderful accompaniment to braised or roasted meats, especially turkey.

1 large beet, scrubbed
1 teaspoon pickling spice
2 bay leaves
2 star anise
1 cinnamon stick
1 cup red wine vinegar
1 teaspoon salt
3 cups water

SACHET
1 teaspoon pickling spice
1 bay leaf
1 cinnamon stick
2 star anise
¼ teaspoon cracked black peppercorns

RELISH
½ cup sugar
1 tablespoon lemon juice
1 small onion, chopped
¼ cup brandy
¼ cup Port
½ cup cranberry juice
¼ cup apple juice
½ cup dried apples, diced
½ cup currant jelly

■ Combine the beet, 1 teaspoon pickling spice, bay leaves, star anise, cinnamon stick, vinegar, salt, and 3 cups water in a nonreactive pot and bring to a boil. Reduce the heat to a simmer and cook until the beet is done but slightly firm, about 50 minutes. Remove beet and refrigerate it. Set aside 1 cup of the cooking liquid, discarding the solids and the remainder of the liquid. When the beet is cool, peel it, and dice it small. Set aside.

- To make the sachet, wrap the pickling spice, bay leaf, cinnamon, star anise, and peppercorns in a square piece of cheesecloth. Pull up the sides and tie with twine to form a small bag.

- Combine the sugar and lemon juice in a nonreactive pot and allow the sugar to turn to amber-brown, without stirring, over medium heat. Immediately add the onion and stir to coat. Remove the pan from the heat. Carefully add the brandy and Port (there will be steam). Stir the mixture, return to the heat, bring to a simmer, and add the sachet. Simmer until the mixture reduces by half. Add the cranberry and apple juice, the apples, currant jelly, and reserved 1 cup of beet cooking juice. Simmer until the apples are soft, remove and discard the sachet, and refrigerate. The mixture should be the consistency of light syrup. If it is too loose, remove the apples and simmer until the proper thickness is reached, then put the apples back into the liquid. Add the diced beets.

- Serve chilled or refrigerate for up to 1 week.

Makes 4½ cups

Corn Pudding

Mark Linden, Glacial Reflections Catering

This recipe uses polenta as the base for a soft corn pudding. Use fresh corn cut from the cob when it's in season instead of frozen corn.

> 1 tablespoon butter, softened
> ¼ cup bread crumbs
> ¼ cup polenta
> 1½ cups frozen corn kernels
> ½ cup milk
> 3 eggs
> 1 teaspoon sugar
> ¼ teaspoon salt
> Pinch of ground black pepper

■ Preheat the oven to 350°F. Grease a small ovenproof pan or Pyrex dish with the butter and coat with the bread crumbs.

■ Cook the polenta in salted water per the instructions on the package.

■ Cook the corn in the milk for 5 minutes. Purée half of the corn-milk mixture and return it to the pot. Stir to recombine.

■ Mix the cooked polenta, corn mixture, eggs, sugar, salt, and pepper in a large bowl. Pour into the pan and bake for 1 hour, or until a toothpick inserted in the center comes out clean. Let sit for 5 minutes.

■ Cut into squares and serve.

Serves four

Glögg

Jens Hansen, Jens' Restaurant and Bodega

This Swedish hot wine is a traditional drink served during the Scandinavian Christmas season. It's perfect for the dark and quite magical holiday season in Alaska. Serve this warming wine drink with roasted chestnuts. *Rigtig God Jul!*

SACHET
3 cinnamon sticks
¼ whole nutmeg, grated
10 whole cloves
¼ teaspoon allspice berries

GLÖGG
1 quart red wine
1 cup sugar
¾ cup aquavit
¾ cup ruby Port
6 tablespoons brandy
Whole blanched almonds
Raisins soaked in wine or Port

■ To make the sachet, wrap the ingredients in a square piece of cheesecloth and tie with twine. Combine the sachet, wine, and sugar in a pot over medium heat and cook until it steams. Add the aquavit, Port, and brandy, stirring. Heat until it steams. This mixture should not boil. Taste and add more sugar if it is to your liking. Remove the sachet when the spice flavors are to your taste.

■ Put 2 to 3 almonds and 1 teaspoon of soaked raisins in a mug or glass and fill with glögg.

Makes about 3½ cups

Alaskan Grape

Diners new to Alaska are often surprised when they stumble across a hard-to-find bottle of California pinot noir or a rare French Bordeaux. One simply doesn't expect to find good wine in a frozen land known for fish and oil. But it's because of the fish and oil that such a wide range of wine can be found in the cellars of some of Alaska's best restaurants.

In the 1970s and early 1980s, oil money flowed freely in bars and restaurants. Oil executives and others from the Lower 48 came north to get in on the boom brought a new sophistication toward wine and the money to pay for it. That helped build the wine cellars at Anchorage restaurants like The Crow's Nest in the Hotel Captain Cook, one of a handful of Alaska restaurants that have won *Wine Spectator* awards for their cellars.

Today, fishing and tourism keep the wine industry buzzing. Hotels from Fairbanks to Juneau tailor their wine offerings to tourists who enjoy good wine. Fishing and hunting lodges, some of which command $3,000 or more a week, stock specials bottles for clients.

At the Marx Bros. Cafe, wine guru Van Hale keeps his cellar stocked with rare wines from California. He often picks up hard-to-find bottles from winemakers who love to come north to fish and eat at the restaurant.

But tourists and good fishing aren't the only reason superb wines can be found in Alaska. The state has plenty of restaurant owners and wine stewards who keep good cellars because they love wine. That's the case at The Corsair in Anchorage, where proprietor Hans Kruger has spent two decades building a cellar that has more than ten thousand bottles, including a six-liter 1979 La Tâche Burgundy.

Black Currant Lemonade

Kirsten Dixon, Riversong Lodge

Black currants can be found throughout Dixon's food. The Experimental Station of the Cooperative Extension Service in Palmer, Alaska, gave Dixon her first black currant bushes. Now there are black currant bushes growing at all of the Dixons' lodges. You may substitute fruit concentrates, such as cranberry or cherry, found in the health food sections of stores.

> 3 cups water
> Zest of 3 lemons
> 2 cups sugar
> 2 cups fresh lemon juice
> ¼ cup black currant concentrate (see page 232)

- Combine the water and lemon zest and bring to a boil. Remove from the heat and stir in the sugar until dissolved. Let stand for 15 minutes.

- Add the lemon juice and currant concentrate and refrigerate until thoroughly chilled. Strain.

- Serve over ice.

> Serves four to six

Sauces, Stocks,
and Other Basics

Blueberry Dijon Vinaigrette

Mark Linden, Glacial Reflections Catering

Salad dressings are simple to make and the possibilities are endless. Local markets now carry a wide variety of vinegars and flavored oils. Always follow a very simple rule: Flavor the vinegar first with all of the ingredients except the oil. Allow the mixture to sit for a few minutes so that all the flavors can develop. Then add the oil of your choice. Be aware that a small percentage of raw egg yolks contain salmonella. If that is a concern, omit the yolks. Without them, the dressing will not stay emulsified as long, and there will be a slight flavor change.

> ½ cup Burgundy or good-quality California red wine
> 3 tablespoons white wine vinegar
> 1 teaspoon chopped shallots
> 1 teaspoon chopped garlic
> ¼ teaspoon ground black pepper
> ½ teaspoon minced rosemary
> ½ cup fresh blueberries or ¾ cup frozen blueberries
> 2 egg yolks
> 1 cup olive oil
> ¼ cup apple juice
> ½ teaspoon salt
> ¼ cup Dijon mustard
> ⅓ cup minced chives

■ Combine the wine, vinegar, shallots, garlic, pepper, rosemary, and blueberries in a medium saucepan over medium heat. Reduce by one fourth, cool, and strain. Set aside.

■ Whisk the yolks in a bowl until pale yellow. Whisking constantly, add the oil in a thin, steady stream, alternating with the apple juice to thin the mixture. When all the oil and apple juice are incorporated, add the salt, mustard, and chives. Add the reserved liquid to the egg mixture, blend well, taste and adjust the seasoning for additional salt and pepper.

■ Serve with a salad of your choice or refrigerate for up to 6 days.

Makes 2 cups

Roasted Red Pepper Vinaigrette

Elizabeth King, Southside Bistro

A strong dressing for sturdy greens.

> 1 roasted red pepper, peeled, seeded, and roughly chopped
> 2 cloves garlic, chopped
> 1 shallot, chopped
> 1 tablespoon Dijon mustard
> 1 tablespoon chopped basil
> ½ tablespoon chopped fresh oregano
> 1 tablespoon chopped Italian parsley
> ½ cup balsamic vinegar
> ¾ cup olive oil
> Salt and ground black pepper

- Combine the red pepper, garlic, shallot, mustard, basil, oregano, parsley, and vinegar in a food processor or blender and process until smooth. With the processor running, add the oil in a slow, steady stream. Season with salt and pepper to taste.

- Serve with a salad of your choice or refrigerate for up to 10 days.

> Makes 2 cups

Roasted Tomato Vinaigrette

Farrokh Larijani, Glacier BrewHouse

This offers a nice change from basic vinaigrettes. Larijani uses it on baby lettuce greens to garnish his Herb-Crusted Halibut (page 86).

½ cup olive oil

¼ cup balsamic vinegar

½ cup Roasted Roma Tomatoes (page 190)

1 tablespoon minced roasted garlic

1 tablespoon minced shallots

¼ teaspoon ground white pepper

¾ teaspoon kosher salt

½ teaspoon fresh thyme leaves

¾ teaspoon minced rosemary

■ Whisk all the ingredients together.

■ Serve with a salad of your choice or refrigerate for up to 10 days.

Makes 1¼ cups

Roasted Roma Tomatoes

Farrokh Larijani, Glacier BrewHouse

Although these tomatoes are used by Larijani in specific recipes in this book, we have adopted (kidnapped) them for other uses as well: on pasta, in turnovers with goat cheese, and on pizza.

> 8 ounces Roma tomatoes, cored and quartered
> 4 tablespoons olive oil
> 2 tablespoons balsamic vinegar
> ¼ teaspoon ground black pepper
> ¾ teaspoon kosher salt

- Preheat the oven to 500°F.

- Toss the tomatoes with the olive oil, vinegar, pepper, and salt in a large bowl.

- Turn into a shallow baking pan and roast for about 20 minutes, or until the edges start to char and the tomatoes form a crust. Let cool in the pan.

- Can be refrigerated for up to 1 week or frozen for up to 2 months. Reheat before serving.

> Makes 8 ounces

Avocado Salsa

Toby Ramey, Sacks Cafe

For fish or simply on fresh tortillas, this salsa has plenty of uses.

> 3 Roma tomatoes, cut into small dice
> ⅓ cup red onion, cut into fine dice
> 1 jalapeño, seeds and ribs removed, cut into fine dice
> 1 avocado, peeled and cut into medium dice
> 2 teaspoons fresh lime juice
> ¼ teaspoon ground cumin
> ¼ teaspoon salt

■ Mix all the ingredients together in a bowl. Adjust seasonings. Chill.

■ Works well with grilled fresh fish. Can be refrigerated for up to 2 days.

> Serves four

Strawberry Vinaigrette

Jens Hansen, Jens' Restaurant and Bodega

Hansen loves this sweet-tart dressing for his salads. It has become a signature at his Anchorage restaurant.

½ cup strawberries, hulled and chopped
¾ cup water
¼ cup red wine vinegar
¾ cup vegetable oil
Salt and ground black pepper
Honey

- Combine the strawberries and water in a medium saucepan over medium-high heat. Bring to a boil, then reduce the heat to maintain a simmer. Reduce by half. Cool.

- Put the vinegar in a medium bowl. Whisking constantly, add the oil in a thin, steady stream. Mix in the strawberry reduction. Season with salt and pepper. Taste, then add honey if it is too tart. Refrigerate.

- Serve with your favorite salad.

Makes 2 cups

Lemon Herb Butter

Farrokh Larijani, Glacier BrewHouse

Here's the perfect topping for any grilled or roasted fish.

12 ounces (3 sticks) salted butter, softened
1 teaspoon grated lemon zest
2 tablespoons fresh lemon juice
1 tablespoon minced shallot
2 tablespoons coarsely chopped chives
¼ cup coarsely chopped basil
2 tablespoons coarsely chopped fresh oregano
¼ cup coarsely chopped parsley
½ teaspoon crushed red pepper

- Beat the softened butter with a mixer until smooth and creamy. Transfer the butter to a food processor. Add all other ingredients and pulse together until incorporated.

- Drizzle over your favorite fish. Can be refrigerated for up to 1 week or frozen for up to 1 month.

Makes 2 cups

Lemon Aïoli

Farrokh Larijani, Orso

This garlic- and lemon-flavored mayonnaise would suit any grilled or roasted seafood. Larijani uses it to garnish his Roasted Salmon with Sauce Verde (page 101). Be aware that a small percentage of raw egg yolks contain salmonella. If that is a concern, omit the yolk. The dressing will not stay emulsified as long, and there will be a slight flavor change.

> 1 egg yolk
> 2 teaspoons chopped garlic
> 1 teaspoon Dijon mustard
> 2 teaspoons white wine vinegar
> ¾ cup olive oil
> 2 tablespoons fresh lemon juice
> ½ teaspoon kosher salt
> Pinch of ground black pepper

■ Put the egg yolk, garlic, mustard, vinegar, and 1 tablespoon of the olive oil in a blender and blend for 1 minute on medium speed. With the blender still on medium speed, add the olive oil in a thin, steady stream. Stop halfway through the process and add the lemon juice. Add the rest of the olive oil with the blender on medium speed. Season with salt and pepper. Refrigerate immediately.

■ Serve with grilled or roasted seafood. Can be refrigerated for up to 1 week.

> Makes 1 cup

Sweet Onion Jam

Elizabeth King, Southside Bistro

This savory jam makes it easy to dress up a simple supper of grilled meat.

3 large sweet onions, such as Walla Walla, very thinly sliced
⅔ cup sugar
½ cup Champagne vinegar
Kosher salt and ground black pepper

■ Place the onions in a large heavy pot and sprinkle with the sugar. Cook over high heat, stirring often to dissolve the sugar. Cook until the onions turn a deep golden brown.

■ Stir in the vinegar and cook until the liquid turns into syrup. Season with salt and pepper to taste. Can be refrigerated for up to 2 weeks.

Makes 3 cups

Salmon or Halibut Marinade for Grilling

Mark Linden, Glacial Reflections Catering

A good all-around marinade for seafood, whether on the grill or broiler.

> 2 tablespoons soy sauce
> ¼ cup rice wine vinegar
> 2 tablespoons peeled and minced fresh ginger
> 1 teaspoon sesame seeds
> 3 tablespoons chopped cilantro
> ½ cup olive oil
> ¼ cup sesame oil

- Combine the soy sauce, vinegar, ginger, sesame seeds, and cilantro. Let rest for 15 minutes.

- Whisk in the olive oil and sesame oil.

- Place the fish in the marinade and marinate for 1 to 2 hours, turning halfway through the process. Drain the fish well. Discard the marinade. Grill or broil fish.

> Makes 1¼ cups

Stocks

Glenn Denkler

A well-prepared stock is what the French call *fond de cuisine* (the foundation of cuisine). It is considered the basic structure around which many fine recipes are built. Most recipes accept canned broth as a substitute, but the extra effort of preparing homemade stock is well worth the trouble. Make lots and freeze it by the pint for future use. Never boil a stock, or it will be cloudy. Before using stock, skim any fat that has risen to the surface. This is very simple once the stock has been refrigerated, because the fat solidifies.

Chicken Stock

> 3 quarts cold water
> 4 pounds chicken bones
> 1 medium onion, peeled and chopped
> 1 carrot, chopped
> 1 stalk celery, chopped
> 1 small leek, white and light green part, chopped
> 1 small bay leaf
> 1 small sprig of thyme or a pinch of dried thyme
> 5 parsley stems
> 5 black peppercorns

- Put the water and bones in a stockpot and bring to a brisk simmer over high heat. Reduce to a slow simmer. Skim the foam as it forms on top of the liquid. Add the onion, carrot, celery, leek, bay leaf, thyme, parsley stems, and peppercorns during the last hour of cooking. Simmer for 4 hours.

- Strain, discard the solids, and cool the stock in an ice bath. Refrigerate or freeze the stock for a later use.

> Makes 2 quarts

Beef Stock

> ¼ cup vegetable oil
> 4 pounds beef bones (veal, pork, or lamb can also be used)
> ½ cup tomato sauce
> 3 quarts cold water
> 1 medium onion, peeled and chopped
> 1 carrot, chopped
> 1 stalk celery, chopped
> 1 small leek, white and light green part, chopped
> 1 small bay leaf
> 1 small sprig of thyme or a pinch of dried thyme
> 5 parsley stems
> 5 black peppercorns

■ Preheat the oven to 400°F.

■ Pour the oil in a roasting pan and place in the oven for 10 minutes. Add the bones, toss, and roast until browned all over. The larger the bones, the longer the roasting time. Add the tomato sauce and roast for 10 minutes more.

■ Remove the bones and tomato sauce from the roasting pan and place them in a large stockpot. Pour off the fat remaining in the pan and set it aside. Add 2 cups of the cold water to the roasting pan. With a wooden spoon, scrape up any brown bits in the pan and add the water mixture to the stockpot. Add remaining cold water to the stockpot and bring to a bare simmer. Skim the foam that rises to the top.

■ Meanwhile, pour the reserved fat back into the roasting pan, add the onion, carrot, celery, and leek. Cook the vegetables on top of the stove over medium-high heat until browned but not burned. Remove the vegetables from the pan and place in the stockpot during the last hour of cooking. Discard any remaining fat in the roasting pan. Ladle a few cups of the stockpot liquid into the roasting pan and scrape up any brown bits. Add the mixture to the stockpot. Return the liquid to a simmer and skim off any foam. Add the bay leaf, thyme, parsley stems, and peppercorns. Simmer chicken for 6 to 8 hours. This should be sufficient time to extract all the flavor from the bones.

■ Strain, discard the solids, and cool stock in an ice bath. Refrigerate or freeze the stock for a later use.

> Makes 2 quarts

Vegetable Stock

2 tablespoons vegetable oil
1 cup sliced white onion
½ cup sliced leek, white and light green part
1 stalk celery, thinly sliced
1 carrot, thinly sliced
½ cup shredded green cabbage
½ cup sliced button mushrooms
4 cloves fresh garlic, sliced
1 cup dry white wine
1 ripe tomato, chopped
4½ quarts cold water
6 black peppercorns
1 star anise
½ cup chopped parsley
1 teaspoon minced fresh thyme leaves
2 tablespoons chopped basil leaves

■ Heat the oil in a large heavy saucepan or small stockpot over medium heat. Add the onion, leek, celery, carrot, cabbage, mushrooms, and garlic. Cook, stirring constantly, until the vegetables are soft. Add the wine, increase the heat, and simmer until the wine is reduced by half. Add the tomato, water, and peppercorns. Bring to a simmer and cook for 45 minutes. Remove the pan from the heat and add the star anise, parsley, thyme, and basil. Let steep for 30 minutes. Cool in an ice bath. Refrigerate for 4 hours, then strain.

■ If not using immediately, refrigerate or freeze.

■ Note: Key elements of this stock are the addition of white wine and the steeping of the herbs. Feel free to add or substitute other herbs to complement the recipe that you will be using the stock in.

Makes 4 quarts

Fish Stock

    1 tablespoon butter

    1 medium onion, peeled and thinly sliced

    1 carrot, thinly sliced

    1 stalk celery, thinly sliced

    1 small leek, white and light green part, thinly sliced

    4 pounds bones (halibut or other mild fish)

    2½ quarts cold water

    1 small bay leaf

    1 small sprig of thyme or a pinch of dried thyme

    5 parsley stems

    5 black peppercorns

■ In a large saucepan, melt butter over medium heat. Add onion, carrot, celery, and leek. Stir vegetables until softened, about 5 minutes. Add bones. Stir until well combined.

■ Add water and increase heat to high. Bring to a simmer and skim off any foam. Add bay leaf, thyme, parsley stems, and peppercorns. Simmer for 45 minutes and then strain. Discard solids.

■ If not using stock immediately, cool in an ice bath. Refrigerate for up to 2 days or freeze for a later use.

    Makes 2 quarts

Shellfish Stock

Jack Amon, Marx Bros. Cafe

This has a distinctive flavor that builds on fish stock. The crushed shells from lobster or crab give the stock depth.

2 tablespoons olive oil
1 pound lobster or crab shells
½ large onion, diced
½ large carrot, diced
2 tablespoons tomato paste
½ cup white wine
2 tablespoons brandy
2 cups cold water or Fish Stock (page 200)
1 stalk celery, chopped
1 bay leaf
1 teaspoon fresh thyme leaves
1 tablespoon chopped parsley
3 cloves garlic
1½ teaspoons black peppercorns
Pinch of cayenne
1½ tablespoons chopped tarragon
2 tablespoons arrowroot powder
¼ cup water
1 tablespoon butter
Salt and ground black pepper

■ Preheat the oven to 375°F.

■ Combine the olive oil and shells in a small roasting pan and roast until the shells are toasted. Crush the shells with a hammer or heavy skillet.

■ Return the shells to the roasting pan. Add the onions and carrots and continue to roast until they are lightly browned. Add the tomato paste and roast for 10 minutes more.

■ Add the wine, brandy, and water to the roasting pan. Scrape any brown bits from the bottom of the pan.

■ Transfer all the roasting pan ingredients to a heavy saucepan. Add the celery, bay leaf, thyme, parsley, garlic, and peppercorns. Bring to a boil, then reduce to a simmer. Cook over low heat for 2 hours. Strain and discard the solids.

- Bring the strained stock to a simmer. Add the cayenne and tarragon. Combine the arrowroot and cold water in a cup and stir until smooth. Whisk the arrowroot mixture into the simmering stock. Remove the saucepan from the heat and whip in the butter.

- Taste and season with salt and pepper to taste.

- If not using immediately, refrigerate or freeze.

Makes 2 cups

Rosemary Jus

Farrokh Larijani, Glacier BrewHouse

This sauce can support roasted meats, punch up roasted or mashed potatoes, or serve as a base for a further-refined sauce.

> 1 tablespoon vegetable oil
> 1½ pounds beef bones
> 8 cups cold water
> 2 ounces au jus mix, preferably Knorr Swiss
> 2 tablespoons soy sauce
> 2 tablespoons Worcestershire sauce
> 1 teaspoon minced garlic
> Pinch of kosher salt
> ½ sprig of rosemary

- Preheat the oven to 450°F.

- Place a roasting pan with oil in the oven to heat for 10 minutes. Remove the pan, add the bones, and stir once. Return the bones to the oven and roast until the bones are well browned, 20 to 30 minutes.

- Transfer the bones from the roasting pan to a stockpot. Discard any oil remaining in the roasting pan. Add 1 cup of water to the pan and scrap up any browned bits. Add the pan juices to the stockpot. Add the remaining water. Simmer for 4 hours. Strain and discard the bones.

- Return the liquid to the stockpot. Add the au jus mix, soy sauce, Worcestershire, garlic, and salt. Simmer 15 minutes. Strain. Add the rosemary to the strained liquid. Transfer to a small pot or bowl and set the pot in an ice-water bath to cool rapidly. When the au jus is cool, remove and discard the rosemary.

- Place the jus in the refrigerator or freeze for a later use.

> Makes 6 cups

Spruce Tip Syrup

David and JoAnn Lesh, Gustavus Inn

Pick the soft, pale green tips of spruce branches in the spring. This syrup is dandy with sourdough pancakes.

> 1½ cups spruce tips
> 1½ cups water
> 1 cup sugar

■ Combine the spruce tips and water in a medium saucepan. Bring to a boil, then reduce to a simmer. Cook for 15 minutes. Strain, setting aside the spruce tea. Add the sugar to the tea. Return this mixture to a boil, then simmer until it reaches desired flavor and consistency.

> Makes about 2 cups

Clarified Butter

Glenn Denkler

Clarified butter is pure butterfat. Because the milk solids and whey are removed, the smoking point is much higher than whole butter. The rich butter and its flavor remain, making it a wonderful sautéing medium.

1 pound unsalted butter

- Melt the butter over medium heat in a heavy saucepan. Skim the foamy milk solids off the surface with a spoon as they appear. Cook until clear. Pour the liquid into a container and refrigerate overnight.

- Poke a couple of holes into the solidified butter and pour out the whey that has settled on the bottom. The butter can be refrigerated, tightly sealed, for up to 2 weeks.

Makes 12 ounces

Desserts

Almond Cake with Raspberry Sauce

Jennifer Jolis, Jennifer's

Many Alaskans spend a lot of time trying to control the wild raspberry and blackberry bushes that threaten to take over roads, lawns, and parks. Others simply enjoy the abundance of berries. The season is short but intense, so many cooks freeze berries to make sure they can have a taste of summer all year. This recipe can be varied depending on the fruit at hand. Any fresh fruit mixed with a simple syrup (a mixture of a cup of sugar and a cup of water simmered until the sugar is dissolved) would be a refreshing treat.

ALMOND CAKE

¾ cup granulated sugar

8 ounces almond paste

8 tablespoons (1 stick) butter, at room temperature

3 eggs

1 tablespoon kirsch (cherry brandy)

¼ teaspoon almond extract

½ teaspoon grated orange zest

¼ cup flour

½ teaspoon baking powder

Powdered sugar, for decoration

RASPBERRY SAUCE

1 package (12 ounces) raspberries in syrup, thawed

1 tablespoon raspberry liqueur or 1 tablespoon cognac plus 1 teaspoon kirsch (liqueur optional)

■ Preheat the oven to 350°F. Butter and flour a 9-inch cake pan. Discard the excess flour. Line the pan with a circle of buttered parchment paper or wax paper. Set aside.

■ To make the almond cake, process the sugar and almond paste in a food processor until finely broken up. Add the butter and process until the dough forms a ball on top of the blade. With the machine running, add the eggs, one at a time, then the kirsch, the almond extract, and the grated zest.

■ Mix the flour and baking powder together in a bowl. Restart the processor, add the flour mixture, and process only just until the flour mixture is incorporated. Pour the batter into the cake pan.

- Bake on the center rack of the oven until a wooden toothpick inserted in the center comes out clean, 35 to 40 minutes. Let stand until cool.

- To make the raspberry sauce, purée the raspberries with their juices in a food processor. Strain through a damp cheesecloth or fine strainer to remove the seeds. Add the liqueur to the puréed raspberries.

- To serve, turn the cake out onto a plate. Sift the powdered sugar over it. Serve with the raspberry sauce.

Serves eight

Apricot Cheesecake

Jennifer Jolis, Jennifer's

This recipe is infinitely adaptable. Consider adding grated lemon and orange zest. Blueberries, frozen or fresh, make a wonderful addition and require no substitutions or deletions. Or replace half a pound of the cream cheese with half a pound of melted white chocolate and 1/4 cup of any liqueur you choose. An easy way to cut cheesecake? Dental floss.

GRAHAM CRACKER CRUST
1 cup graham cracker crumbs
3 tablespoons butter, melted
1 teaspoon ground cinnamon
1/4 cup sugar

APRICOT FILLING
1 cup dried apricots
2 tablespoons Cognac
2 1/4 pounds cream cheese, softened
1 cup sugar
1 tablespoon vanilla extract
4 eggs

- Preheat the oven to 300°F.

- To make the crust, combine graham cracker crumbs, butter, cinnamon, and sugar in a bowl. Press into the bottom and up the sides of a 9-inch springform pan. Bake for 10 minutes and remove. Set aside.

- For the filling, cover the apricots with water by 1 inch in a small saucepan. Bring to a boil, then reduce to a simmer. Cook until the apricots are tender. Drain and discard the excess water. Purée the apricots in a food processor. Add the Cognac and process until incorporated. Remove and set aside.

- Beat the cream cheese with a heavy-duty mixer, using the paddle, until it is light and fluffy. Add the sugar and vanilla. Beat on low speed until just incorporated. Add the eggs, one at a time, on low speed, beating a little between each addition.

- Pour half the batter into the crust. Using a large spoon, carefully spread spoonfuls of the reserved apricot purée into the batter. Be careful not to allow the apricot to come in contact with the sides of the pan. Add the remainder of the batter to the pan, and smooth the surface.

■ Bake the cheesecake in the oven for 1½ hours, or until the top of the cake feels dry to the touch, but the center is not yet firm. Remove the cheesecake from the oven and let it cool at room temperature before placing it in the refrigerator. Chill for at least 6 hours before serving.

Makes one 9-inch cheesecake

Apple Crisp

JoAnn Asher, Sacks Cafe

Apples don't grow well in Alaska, but they ship and store well. Several varieties can be found at the grocery store or in Anchorage's summer farmers' market. The beauty of this recipe is its simplicity. It also lends itself to modification. Exchange some apples for fresh pears. Instead of Triple Sec, try another liquor such as peach brandy. It is foolproof.

APPLE FILLING
5 Granny Smith apples, peeled, cored, and sliced
¼ teaspoon ground cinnamon
½ teaspoon chopped lemon zest
1½ teaspoons Triple Sec
1½ teaspoons sugar
¼ cup dried tart cherries

TOPPING
⅓ cup granulated sugar
2 tablespoons (packed) brown sugar
⅓ cup flour
Pinch of salt
2 tablespoons butter, chilled, cut into small pieces

- Preheat the oven to 350°F.

- To make the apple filling, toss all the ingredients in a large bowl, then transfer to an 8 x 6-inch pan or ovenproof glass dish.

- To make the topping, process all the ingredients in a food processor until coarsely ground and crumbly. Do not overprocess. Sprinkle on top of apple mixture.

- Bake until the apples are tender and the top is light brown, about 1 hour.

- Serve warm.

Serves six

Baked Alaska

Kirsten Dixon, Riversong Lodge

Dixon has been preparing variations on this theme for years. People seem to expect it from an Alaska chef. Most food scholars believe the dish was invented in the 1860s or '70s to commemorate the United States purchase of Alaska from Russia. Dixon likes to press edible wildflowers around the outside of the ice cream and sometimes sprinkles bee pollen onto the plates for added flavor and color. She has a commercial ice cream maker at Winterlake Lodge to make lots of different types of ice creams. She also has her own laying hens, so she doesn't worry about salmonella and therefore doesn't heat the meringue. When she is at a public event or not using her own eggs, however, she always uses the heated method.

> 8 slices (½ inch each) pound or angel food cake
> 1 pint vanilla ice cream, softened
> ½ cup granulated sugar
> 2 egg whites
> ¼ teaspoon cream of tartar
> ½ teaspoon vanilla extract
> 1 tablespoon crème de cassis
> ¼ cup mixed fresh berries, such as blueberries and raspberries

■ Chill 4 small dessert plates.

■ Using a 3-inch round cutter, cut 8 circles from the cake slices. Set four of the rounds at least 3 inches apart on a baking sheet lined with parchment paper or plastic wrap. Top each with a scoop of ice cream. Lightly press a second round of cake on top of each scoop. With a palette knife or small butter knife, spread more ice cream smoothly around the sides. Cover with plastic wrap and freeze at least 15 minutes to firm the cakes.

■ Bring about 1 inch of water to a simmer in a large saucepan. Put the sugar, egg whites, 2 tablespoons water, and the cream of tartar in a metal bowl that will fit over the saucepan. Set the bowl over the water and beat with an electric mixer at low speed for 3 to 5 minutes, or until an instant-read thermometer registers 140°F. Increase the mixer speed to high and continue beating over the heat for a full 3 minutes. Remove the bowl from the heat and beat the meringue until cool, about 4 minutes. Beat in the vanilla. Cover with plastic wrap and put in the refrigerator to chill for at least 15 minutes.

- When ready to assemble, preheat the broiler.

- Cover the cakes with the meringue, using a pastry bag or palette knife to make decorative swirls and ensure that the meringue covers the cake completely.

- Immediately place the cakes under the broiler as close to the heat as possible until the meringue is lightly browned, about 1 minute. A hand-held torch may be used instead to brown the meringue.

- Drizzle the crème de cassis onto the dessert plates. Place each baked Alaska in the center of a plate. Sprinkle each plate with fresh berries.

Serves four

Warm Berry Crisp with Birch Syrup Butter Pecan Ice Cream

Jack Amon, Marx Bros. Cafe

This is one of the favorite desserts served at the Marx Bros. Cafe. Birch syrup can be ordered from Kahiltna Birchworks in Alaska (see page 232), or you may substitute good-quality pure maple syrup. David Lesh's Spruce Tip Syrup (page 204) would also be worth a try.

BERRY FILLING
6 cups mixed fruits, such as berries, peaches, nectarines, and/or apples
¼ cup granulated sugar
2 tablespoons flour

CRUMB TOPPING
¾ cup flour
⅓ cup (firmly packed) light brown sugar
⅓ cup granulated sugar
¼ teaspoon salt
¼ teaspoon ground cinnamon
⅛ teaspoon ground ginger
6 tablespoons (¾ stick) butter
Birch Syrup Butter Pecan Ice Cream (page 217)

- Preheat the oven to 400°F.

- To make the berry filling, combine the fruit, sugar, and flour. Pour into a 9-inch square baking dish.

- To make the crumb topping, mix the flour, brown sugar, granulated sugar, salt, cinnamon, and ginger in a medium bowl. Add the butter and cut it in with 2 knives or a pastry cutter until the mixture resembles coarse meal.

- Spread the crumb topping over the filling. Bake for 20 to 30 minutes, or until the top is browned and the juices are bubbling around the edges.

- Remove from the oven and let cool for at least 15 minutes before serving.

- Cut into 3-inch squares. Top with ice cream.

    Serves nine

Birch Syrup Butter Pecan Ice Cream

> 6 egg yolks
> ½ cup birch syrup or good-quality pure maple syrup with
>   a little maple extract
> ½ cup (firmly packed) light brown sugar
> 1½ cups milk
> 1½ cups heavy cream
> 2 tablespoons butter
> ¼ cup pecan pieces

■ Whisk together the egg yolks, birch syrup, and brown sugar in a large bowl.
Set aside.

■ Heat the milk and cream to a bare simmer in a heavy saucepan. Gradually whisk
the milk mixture into the yolk mixture. Place the bowl over a saucepan of simmering water. Cook, stirring constantly, until the mixture coats the back of a wooden
spoon. Remove from the heat and set the bowl into a larger bowl of ice. Stir until
it starts to cool. Let it rest on the ice.

■ Melt the butter in a small skillet over medium heat. Add the pecans and cook for
3 minutes. Remove from the heat and set aside.

■ Place the cooled custard in an ice cream machine and begin the freezing process.
When the custard is almost set, add the pecans and finish freezing.

> Makes 2½ pints

Chocolate Brownies with Blueberries

Kirsten Dixon, Winterlake Lodge

This recipe has become a staple all year long at Winterlake Lodge. Dixon and her crew send the heli-skiers and hikers out with brownies in their packed lunches during the summer; dog mushers sled out with them in their trail snacks in the winter. The drizzled crème de cassis adds texture and color contrast to the tops of the brownies.

10 ounces semisweet chocolate, chopped
12 ounces (3 sticks) butter
6 eggs
3 cups sugar
2 teaspoons vanilla extract
1 teaspoon kosher salt
2 cups plus 2 tablespoons cake flour
2 cups coarsely chopped walnuts
2 cups frozen blueberries or mixed berries
3 tablespoons crème de cassis

- Preheat the oven to 275°F. Butter an 18 x 12-inch jelly-roll pan and line it with parchment paper. Set aside.

- Melt the chocolate and butter in a double boiler.

- Beat the eggs, sugar, and vanilla with a mixer on medium speed until light and fluffy. Stir the chocolate mixture into the egg mixture. Fold 2 cups of the flour into the chocolate-egg mixture. Stir in the nuts.

- Toss the berries in the remaining 2 tablespoons flour and fold into the brownie mixture. Spread the mixture in the pan. Drizzle the crème de cassis over the top of the brownie mixture.

- Bake for 30 to 40 minutes, or until the brownies are firm in the center. Do not overbake. Cool the pan on a rack. Cut the brownies into 2-inch squares.

Makes 54 small brownies

Chocolate Raspberry Torte

David and JoAnn Lesh, Gustavus Inn

The food at the Lesh's lodge is simple, but it has to have a sophisticated edge to appeal to many of the well-traveled guests who stay there. This simple torte is best with fresh raspberries, but frozen ones also work nicely.

2 ounces unsweetened chocolate, chopped small
¼ cup boiling water
4 ounces (1 stick) salted butter
1 cup granulated sugar
2 egg yolks
½ teaspoon vanilla extract
1 cup plus 2 tablespoons flour
½ teaspoon baking soda
⅓ cup buttermilk
2 egg whites
¼ teaspoon salt
1 cup heavy cream
2 tablespoons sifted powdered sugar
½ cup frozen raspberries in juice, thawed (or fresh)
Fresh raspberries
Mint leaves

- Preheat the oven to 350°F. Lightly spray a 10-inch cake pan with a removable bottom with vegetable oil or wipe lightly with vegetable oil or shortening. Set aside.

- Mix the chocolate and boiling water in a small bowl and stir until the chocolate is melted. Set aside.

- Cream together the butter and granulated sugar with a mixer until light and fluffy. On slow speed, beat in the egg yolks, vanilla, and melted chocolate.

- Sift together the flour and baking soda. Blend the flour mixture and buttermilk into the butter-chocolate mixture alternately until just combined.

- Beat the egg whites and salt by hand in a clean bowl with a whisk until soft peaks form. Gently fold the whites into the batter by hand. Pour the batter into the pan.

- Bake in the center of the oven for 35 minutes, or until a wooden toothpick inserted into the center of the cake comes out clean. Cool the cake on a rack.

■ Remove the cake from the pan. Split the cake horizontally in half with a bread knife.

■ Whip the cream to soft peaks with the powdered sugar. Fold in the raspberries. This is the raspberry fool.

■ Spread one third of the fool on the bottom half of the cake. Place the top half of the cake on top of the fool. Spread the remaining fool on the top and sides of the cake.

■ Slice the cake and garnish with fresh raspberries and mint leaves.

Makes one 10-inch torte

Chocolate Zucchini Cake

David and JoAnn Lesh, Gustavus Inn

Grated carrots or parsnips work as well as the zucchini, so feel free to substitute them as long as the total is three cups. This is a very rich cake that needs no frosting.

4 ounces unsweetened chocolate, chopped
3 cups all-purpose flour
1½ teaspoons baking powder
1½ teaspoons baking soda
1 teaspoon salt
1 cup nuts, such as pecans or walnuts, chopped
4 eggs
1½ cups vegetable oil
3 cups sugar
3 cups grated zucchini

■ Preheat the oven to 350°F.

■ Melt the chocolate in a metal bowl over steaming water. Remove from the heat and set aside.

■ Sift together the flour, baking powder, baking soda, and salt. Stir in the nuts. Set aside.

■ Beat the eggs and oil together in a mixer on high speed until fluffy. Stir in the sugar. Fold in the chocolate. Fold together the flour mixture, the chocolate mixture, and the zucchini. Pour the batter into a 14 x 9-inch cake pan and bake for 45 minutes to 1 hour, or just until the cake springs back to a light touch. Let cool in the pan before slicing.

Makes one 14 x 9-inch cake

Chocolate Truffle Torte

Jack Amon, Marx Bros. Cafe

For chocolate lovers everywhere. This simple recipe will satisfy those mid-winter cravings.

> 4 ounces semisweet chocolate, cut into bits
> 3 ounces (¾ stick) butter, cut into bits
> ¾ cup granulated sugar
> 1½ tablespoons cornstarch
> 2 extra large eggs
> 2 egg yolks
> 1½ teaspoons Grand Marnier
> Cocoa powder, for dusting
> Powdered sugar, for dusting
> Chocolate Sauce (page 223)
> Vanilla ice cream

- Place the chocolate and butter in a metal bowl, heat over steaming water, and stir until melted.

- Whisk together the sugar and cornstarch in a bowl. Add the chocolate mixture and stir until smooth. Whisk together the eggs, yolks, and Grand Marnier. Stir into chocolate mixture until combined. Cover and refrigerate 8 hours or overnight.

- Heat the oven to 375°F. Butter an 8-inch tart pan with a removable bottom. Line with parchment paper, then butter the paper. Coat with cocoa powder.

- Fill the pan with the batter. Bake for 20 minutes. Let cool for 5 minutes.

- Invert the cake onto a plate and carefully unmold. Divide the cake into 4 portions and place each on a separate plate. Dust the top of each portion with powdered sugar and garnish with chocolate sauce and vanilla ice cream.

Serves four

Chocolate Sauce

    1 cup heavy cream
    2 tablespoons light corn syrup or honey
    7 ounces bittersweet chocolate, chopped
    ¼ teaspoon vanilla

- In a medium saucepan over medium heat, bring the heavy cream and corn syrup (or honey) to a simmer. Remove from heat. Add the chocolate and vanilla. Stir with a wooden spoon until the chocolate is melted. Keep warm over a warm (not boiling) water bath.

- Tightly cover any leftover sauce and refrigerate for up to 1 week. Reheat over a warm-water bath.

    Makes 1 pint

Danish Christmas Rice Pudding

Jens Hansen, Jens' Restaurant and Bodega

A definite party favorite during the holidays, but it's not low-fat dessert. Kiaffa is a Danish wine that comes in many flavors, including chocolate. Hansen chooses cherry for the sauce to go with this pudding.

RICE PUDDING
1¼ cups medium- or short-grain rice
11 cups heavy cream
¾ cup almonds, chopped
1 cup sugar
1 tablespoon vanilla extract
3 envelopes gelatin
1 cup hot water

CHERRY SAUCE
3 cups cherry Kiaffa
2 cups cherry juice
¼ cup cornstarch
1 package (12 ounces) frozen cherries

- To make the rice pudding, place the rice and 9 cups of the cream in a large pot. Bring to a boil, then reduce to a bare simmer. Cook gently until the rice is tender to the bite, about 20 minutes. Remove from the heat. Add the almonds, sugar, and vanilla.

- Dissolve the gelatin in the hot water, add to the rice mixture, and blend. Cool.

- Whip the remaining 2 cups of cream to soft peaks. When the rice mixture is cool, but not stiff, fold in the whipped cream.

- To make the cherry sauce, heat the Kiaffa and cherry juice to a simmer. Add just enough cold water to the cornstarch to make a slurry. Whip the cornstarch slurry into the Kiaffa mixture in a steady stream. Add the cherries and simmer until the cherries are heated through.

- Serve the hot cherry sauce over the pudding.

Serves sixteen

Einstein's Espresso

Jennifer Jolis, Jennifer's

Jennifer's husband, Daniel, ordered this at one of their favorite restaurants in Portland, Zefiro's. There the name is in Italian, but the idea seemed so simple—so universal and so brilliant—that she credits it to Einstein.

> 8 scoops good-quality ice cream, vanilla or chocolate
> 8 shots freshly brewed espresso
> 8 tablespoons whipped cream
> 4 chocolate-covered espresso beans

■ For each serving, place 2 scoops of ice cream in a tall ice-cream-soda glass. Repeat with 3 more glasses. Pour the espresso equally among the glasses. Top each with whipped cream and an espresso bean. Serve each with a long spoon and 2 straws.

Serves four

Kitty's Cheesecake

David and JoAnn Lesh, Gustavus Inn

The cheesecake may be garnished with thickened and sweetened red currant juice and mint leaves.

1 egg
½ cup flour
2 tablespoons plus ⅔ cup plus 2 tablespoons sugar
4 ounces (1 stick) plus butter
1¼ pounds cream cheese
2 eggs
1½ teaspoons vanilla extract
2 tablespoons fresh lemon juice
1 cup sour cream or yogurt

- Preheat the oven to 350°F.

- Separate the egg and set the white aside. Beat the egg yolk, flour, 2 tablespoons of the sugar, and the butter with a wooden spoon until well blended. Press the mixture into the bottom of a 10-inch springform pan, using the egg white on your fingers to keep the crust from sticking to them. Bake for 10 minutes, then remove from the oven. Cool.

- While the crust is baking, cream the cream cheese, ⅔ cup of the sugar, the 2 whole eggs, 1 teaspoon of the vanilla, and the lemon juice. Pour on top of cooled crust. Bake for 25 minutes.

- While the cheesecake is baking, mix the sour cream, the remaining 2 tablespoons sugar, and the remaining ½ teaspoon vanilla. When the cheesecake is done, spread this mixture over the cheesecake. Bake for 25 more minutes. Remove from the oven and refrigerate for at least 2 hours before serving.

Makes one 10-inch cheesecake

Lemon Meringue Pie
with Raspberries

David and JoAnn Lesh, Gustavus Inn

The addition of fresh raspberries lifts this pie to a higher level of fun. Try other fresh berries as they come into season.

1 cup granulated sugar
5 tablespoons cornstarch
Pinch of salt
2 cups water
3 eggs
3 tablespoons butter
Grated zest of 2 lemons
⅓ cup fresh lemon juice
1½ cups fresh raspberries
1 blind-baked 10-inch pie shell, cooled
1 teaspoon cream of tartar
½ cup sifted powdered sugar

■ Mix together the granulated sugar, cornstarch, and salt in a heavy saucepan. Add the water and mix well. Bring to a boil, then reduce the heat to a simmer. Cook for 5 minutes.

■ Separate the eggs and set the whites aside. Whisk the egg yolks in a small bowl until light. Whisking constantly, add ½ cup of the hot sugar mixture in a thin stream. Whisk the egg yolk mixture slowly back into the hot sugar mixture remaining in the saucepan. Simmer for 3 minutes. Add the butter, lemon zest, and lemon juice to the saucepan and stir until the butter melts and all the ingredients are combined.

■ Spread the raspberries on the cooled pie shell. Cover the raspberries with the hot lemon mixture. Refrigerate for at least 2 hours.

■ Preheat the oven to 350°F about 1½ hours before serving the pie.

■ Whip the reserved egg whites in a clean mixing bowl on medium speed until foamy. Add the cream of tartar and powdered sugar. Whip on medium-high speed until the whites form soft peaks. Spread the meringue on top of the chilled pie. Place in the oven for 15 minutes until the meringue is light brown. Cool on a rack at room temperature.

Makes one 10-inch pie

Lemon Pots de Crème

Margie Brown, Sacks Cafe

Out of time and ideas for a quick and elegant dessert? Be dangerous and substitute orange and/or lime for the lemon.

> 1 to 2 lemons, depending on size
> ⅔ cup sugar
> 1 egg
> 4 egg yolks
> 1¼ cups heavy cream

- Preheat the oven to 325°F.

- Grate the lemon(s) and set aside 1 teaspoon of the zest. Juice the lemon(s); you should have ½ cup. Set aside.

- Whisk the sugar into the egg and egg yolks until light and smooth. Add the lemon juice, cream, and zest and whisk until smooth. Divide the mixture among 4 ramekins.

- Place the ramekins in a baking tray at least 1 inch deep. Pour hot water around the ramekins until the water level is halfway up the side of the ramekins. Bake for about 50 minutes, or until just set.

- Serve warm.

> Serves four

Yukon Sourdough Bread Pudding

Al Levinsohn, Alyeska Resort

Bread pudding is a perfect way to use up stale bread and make you smile at the same time. This variation transcends other pretenders, and the sourdough and Yukon Jack give it a decidedly Alaska feel.

 1 tablespoon butter
 2 cups heavy cream
 ⅔ cup granulated sugar
 ⅓ vanilla bean
 4 egg yolks
 8-ounce loaf sourdough bread, stale
 1 medium Gala apple, peeled, cored, and diced
 ¼ cup currants
 1¼ teaspoons ground cinnamon
 ¼ teaspoon ground nutmeg
 3 tablespoons (packed) light brown sugar
 1 tablespoon Yukon Jack liqueur
 Yukon Jack Sauce (page 230)

■ Preheat the oven to 350°F. Butter a small ovenproof glass baking dish.

■ To make a batter, mix together the cream, sugar, and vanilla bean in a small saucepan and heat until tiny bubbles appear around the edges. Remove from the heat. Very slowly whisk the hot liquid into the egg yolks. Refrigerate if not using immediately.

■ Cut the bread loaf in half and immerse in the batter to moisten. Squeeze lightly to remove excess batter and transfer to a large bowl. Tear the bread into roughly 1-inch pieces. Add the apple, currants, cinnamon, nutmeg, brown sugar, and Yukon Jack and mix well. Add the batter and mix well. Place the mixture in the buttered dish. Bake for about 45 minutes, or until an instant-read thermometer registers 170°F.

■ Top each serving with 2 tablespoons of the Yukon Jack sauce and serve.

 Serves eight

Yukon Jack Sauce

1 egg
⅔ cup sugar
¼ cup heavy cream
2 ounces (½ stick) butter
2 tablespoons Yukon Jack

■ Whisk together the egg and sugar in a bowl until light and smooth, and set aside. Combine the cream, butter, and Yukon Jack and heat gently until small bubbles appear around the edge of the pan. Remove the saucepan from the heat

■ Slowly whisk the hot cream mixture into the egg mixture until combined.

■ Put the mixture back into the saucepan. Stirring constantly, heat gently until the mixture is thick enough to coat the back of a spoon.

■ Serve warm.

Serves eight

Appendix: The Restaurants

Alyeska Resort
1000 Arlberg Avenue
Girdwood, Alaska 99587
(907) 754-1111
food@alyeskaresort.com
www.alyeskaresort.com

Fiddlehead Restaurant and
Bakery
429 West Willoughby Avenue
Juneau, Alaska 99801
(907) 586-3150
fiddlehead@alaska.net
www.alaska.net/~fiddle/

Glacial Reflections Catering
630 West Fourth Avenue
Anchorage, Alaska 99501
(907) 334-9000
www.alaskan.com/glacialreflections/

Glacier BrewHouse
737 West Fifth Avenue
Anchorage, Alaska 99504
(907) 274-2739
www.glacierbrewhouse.com/

Gustavus Inn
P.O. Box 60
Gustavus, Alaska 99826
(907)697-2254 or
(800) 649-5220
dave@gustavusinn.com
www.gustavusinn.com/

The Homestead
Mile 8.2 East End Road
Homer, Alaska 99603
(907) 235-8723

Jens' Restaurant and Bodega
701 West 36th Avenue
Anchorage, Alaska 99503
(907) 561-5367
jens@alaska.net

Marx Bros. Cafe
627 West Third Avenue
Anchorage, Alaska 99501
(907) 278-2133
marx_bros@compuserve.com
www.marxcafe.com

Orso
737 Fifth Avenue
Anchorage, Alaska 99504
(907) 222-3232

Sacks Cafe
328 G Street
Anchorage, Alaska 99501
(907) 274-4022
sacks1@alaska.com
www.sackscafe.com

Southside Bistro
1320 Huffman Park Drive
Anchorage, Alaska 99515
(907) 348-0088

Within the Wild Lodges
(Riversong Lodge, Winterlake Lodge,
and Redoubt Bay Lodge)
2463 Cottonwood Street
Anchorage, Alaska 99508
(907) 274-2710
alaskawild@gci.net
www.withinthewild.com

Appendix: Food Resources

Alaska Seafood

New Sagaya International
Market
3700 Old Seward Highway
Anchorage, Alaska 99503
(907) 561-5173
(800) 764-1001
seafood@newsagaya.com
www.newsagaya.com

Deep Creek Custom Packing
Mile 137 Sterling Highway
P.O. Box 229
Ninilchick, Alaska 99639
(907) 567-3395
(800) 764-0078
dccp@ptialaska.net
www.deepcreekcustompacking.com/

Information about Alaska Seafood and More Recipes

Alaska Seafood Marketing
Institute
311 North Franklin Street
Suite 200
Juneau, Alaska 99801
(907) 465-5560
(800) 478-2903
www.alaskaseafood.org/

Alaska Game Meat

Indian Valley Meats
H.C. 52, P.O. Box 8809
Indian, Alaska
(907) 653-7511
www.indianvalleymeats.com/

Alaska Game & Gourmet
(907) 278-8500

Other Alaskan Food Products

Fresh & Wild
(Black currant concentrate)
(800) 222-5578

Kahiltna Birchworks
(Alaska birch syrup)
(800) 380-7457
alaskabirchsyrup.com

Tamale Wrappers and Other Ethnic Foods

EthnicGrocer.com

Demi-Glace and Other Gourmet Foods

Dean & Deluca
(800) 221-7714
www.dean-deluca.com

Williams-Sonoma
(800) 541-2233
www.williams-sonoma.com

Index

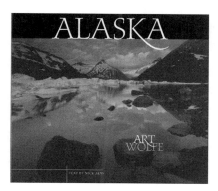
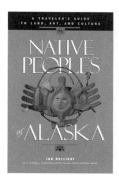

About the Authors

Photo by Sheryl Davis

Kim Severson

Kim Severson spent most of the 1990s writing about Alaska restaurants and food for the *Anchorage Daily News*, the state's largest daily newspaper. She was also an editor for the newspaper, working both on the features desk and the city desk. She now lives in Berkeley, California, and works as a restaurant critic, food writer, and editor at the *San Francisco Chronicle*. She also writes for national magazines. Her writing has won several awards, including the James Beard Award for feature writing and top honors from the Association of Sunday and Features Editors, the Association of American Food Writers, and the Society of Professional Journalists. This is her first cookbook.

Glenn Denkler

After working in several restaurants and graduating first in his class from the Culinary Institute of America, Glenn Denkler moved to Alaska in 1985 and took over as executive chef of Josephine's in the Sheraton Anchorage Hotel. He then moved into education, and is chef instructor at the King Career Center for the Anchorage School District. He is a member of the University of Alaska Culinary Arts Advisory Board and an office holder in the American Culinary Federation–Alaska Culinary Association. He was voted Alaska Chef of the Year in 1993 and 1996.

Bro. Brian